Philosophy for Everyman

Philosophy
for
Everyman

By

Dagobert D. Runes

1974

LITTLEFIELD, ADAMS & CO.
Totowa, New Jersey

Published 1974 by
LITTLEFIELD, ADAMS & CO.

by arrangement with Philosophical Library, Inc.

Library of Congress Cataloging in Publication Data

Runes, Dagobert David, 1902—
  Philosophy for Everyman

  (A Littlefield, Adams Quality Paperback No. 276)
  1. Philosophy—History.   2. Philosophers.
I. Title.
[B72.R75 1974]   109   74-3082
ISBN 0-8226-0276-8

Printed in the United States of America

Contents

THALES

Thales of Miletus (*ca.* 600 B.C.) is generally considered the first philosopher of Western civilization. He was reputed by the ancients to have been widely traveled and highly learned, and was counted among "the seven wise men" of Greece. He does, in fact, seem to have been acquainted with both Egyptian and Babylonian astronomy. But what we have of his limited knowledge hardly supports the claim that he once predicted an eclipse.

We know little of Thales' philosophy, for none of his writings have survived—if, indeed, he ever made a written record of his thoughts. According to Aristotle,[1] Thales believed that it was water "which existed before all existing things came to be, out of which all things came and into which all things return." He pictured the earth as a flat disc swimming on the surface of a boundless expanse of water. He believed that the world was filled with animate beings, and his awareness of electric attraction led him to attribute souls even to magnets.

ANAXIMANDER

Anaximander (611-547 B.C.), a compatriot and contemporary of Thales, is called "the Father of Metaphysics." Only a few lines, and not one complete sentence, remain of his treatise, *On Nature*, a title which has since become a classic for philosophic works. His truly philosophic or chemico-physical theories are therefore very uncertain. The beginning and cause of all the worlds he names *"apeiron,"* which can be translated as "the uncertain" or "the unbounded."[2] Along with this obscure definition, Anaximan-

1

der states that this universal substratum is in constant motion, so that the opposing qualities within it divide and are separated out. His views in brief: Our world was generated by such a process of separating the opposites from the unbounded. At first the "cold" and the "hot" separated. These in turn created humidity, the primal substance, of which the highest form is the sea. Out of this original humidity, in turn, were separated the earth, the air and a sort of pillar of flame, the latter two circling the first.[3] Then the pillar of flame broke apart, and the sun, moon and stars were formed. The flaming pillar was forced into a great number of holes in the spheres, made of compressed air and driven horizontally around the earth by the wind. Earth itself has a cylindrical form. Its original substance was liquid, and in the process of evaporation by the sun, it gave birth to animals and men.

ANAXIMENES

The following fragment is all that remains of the theories of natural law held by the third Miletian philosopher, Anaximenes (*ca.* 550 B.C.): "Just as the air which is our soul surrounds us, so do the wind and air encompass the world."[4] Evidently the indeterminateness of Anaximander's world substance did not satisfy Anaximenes, while he seems to have preferred air to the water of Thales because of its greater fluidity and capacity for expansion.

Anaximenes explains the creation of fire out of air as a process of thinning out, or rarefication; on the other hand, a process of thickening, or condensation, produced water, the earth, the sun, etc. Thus, according to Anaximenes, the density of a body bears a direct relation to its temperature. Of the earth he said that it hung like a disc in the air. He said the same of the sun, which in appearance reminded him of a flat leaf. In contrast, he described the moon and stars as nails driven into the firmament.

The creation of the stars he explained as a process in

which the moisture of the earth was evaporated, or rarefied, back into fire. The sun was drawn earthward, attaining its white heat through the rapidity of its motion. He described the sun's path as circular over the earth, rather than around it. It is invisible at times because it is concealed from sight by high mountains in the north.

This is virtually the sum of our knowledge of the philosophy of Anaximenes.

DIOGENES OF APOLLONIA

About 425 B.C., a champion of Anaximenes' theory of air as the primary substance appeared in the person of Diogenes of Apollonia. Diogenes followed his master's view that all matter was a transmutation of air, the change consisting of a relative rarefication or condensation of this primal substance.

Because the denser substance sank, two masses took form which, whirling under the influence of fire, formed the stars and the earth. Furthermore, it is the air which gives both men and animals the power of motion.[5] Diogenes classified the air under various categories. Soul air, for instance, is finer and warmer than body air, while sun air is warmer than soul air.

HIPPON

Hippon (*ca.* 550 B. C.) agreed with Thales that humidity was the primary substance, pointing to the humidity of the sperm in support of his contention. According to his view, fire was made from water, and the world was created by the subsequent action of the fire upon the water. Like the other Ionic philosophers, Hippon assumed a periodic creation of the universe.

3

HERACLITUS

Heraclitus of Ephesus (*ca.* 500 B.C.) is the most stimulating of the pre-Socratic philosophers. Through lack of aggressiveness on his part and the ingratitude of his countrymen, he relinquished his inherited position of honor as high priest and went into seclusion, contemptuous of the masses that "did not understand even if it perceived. . . . They are like the deaf." All his personal utterances reflect disillusion and bitterness, and what we know of his behavior confirms this pessimism and skepticism. In contrast to Democritus, "the Laughing Philosopher," Heraclitus was known as "the Weeping Philosopher." His contemporaries also called him "Skoteinos" ("the Dark One") because his style was too involved for them to follow, and his relations with his fellow philosophers were mainly unfriendly. He said of Homer that he deserved to be whipped.

Heraclitus' comments on the flux of life and the struggle in nature have been greatly overestimated by modern historians of philosophy. Such an observation as, "Who rises in the same stream will always struggle with fresh waters," makes too little precise sense for us to attach great importance to it. The habit of imbuing such naive reflections with profound meanings is uncritical and certainly unjust to the philosopher. Like all thinkers of his time, Heraclitus faced reality with a profound awareness of his own helplessness.

He taught that the world is composed of three substances: fire, water and earth. These pass from one into another in a regular order of mutation: on the one hand, fire changes to water and water to earth; on the other, earth changes to water and water back into fire. Thus water divides, one half to form earth, the other half, fire. The source of Heraclitus' theory of an upward- and downward-streaming substance remains unknown to us.

In another context Heraclitus said that fire was the primary cause of the world as well as "the principle of world logic." For this reason, the fiery, dry soul is more nearly perfect than the humid one, while "it is death for the soul to turn into water." Whence arises his judgment that the drunkard is seriously imperfect because "his soul is wet."

Heraclitus visualized the sun as being the size of a plate (or, in another simile, as broad as a man's foot), and evidently believed that it was extinguished and relit daily. He conceived of the heavens as mighty vaults rotating around the earth, with openings in which vapor rising from the ocean had gathered and formed the sun and solar system.

Heraclitus strove to give a scientific explanation to natural phenomena, but as with all early Greek philosophers, his efforts were handicapped by the inadequate cosmogony and physics of his time. The Stoics later based their beliefs on Heraclitean physics, and among modern philosophers, Hegel acknowledges a debt to the philosophy of Heraclitus.

The chain of Hylozoists ends with Heraclitus. From the representatives included here it is clear that they conceived their first obligation to be the explanation of nature in terms of a primary substance. Their lack of exact knowledge and sound scientific method made it impossible for them to go beyond vague speculations, grounded in superstition, which were to exercise a persistent and often destructive influence on the minds of succeeding generations.

Their philosophic "systems" were built, not on scientific investigation and logical study, but on fragmentary observations of nature and inaccurate conclusions. In attempting to develop a physics, the Hylozoists gave birth to a metaphysics. For that which would have required demonstrable proof in physics, they could state boldly and without inhibition in metaphysics.

XENOPHANES

About 540 B.C. an evil-mocker appeared among the Greeks in the person of Xenophanes of Colophon. With devastating sarcasm he scourged the ignorance, egotism and pride of the people, and the blind adoration they lavished on everything that was primitive but powerful. He composed a series of lyric, epic and didactic poems, without (so Aristotle complained) committing himself to any definite position or point of view.

His work contains many evidences of protest against popular religious beliefs—not, as has often been maintained, against the polytheism of the Greek cults, but rather against the distorted anthropomorphism to which they were addicted. "Homer and Hesiod," he accused, "have attributed to the gods everything which is blameworthy in the eyes of men, stealing, adultery and mutual deception." He noted, aptly: "If oxen, horses or lions were able to draw pictures as men do, oxen would draw gods that were oxlike, horses gods that were horselike, and lions lionlike gods. . . . The Ethiopians say the gods are black and flat-nosed, while the Thracians declare they are blue-eyed and redheaded."

But while Xenophanes opposed anthropomorphism, other of his statements, of unquestioned authenticity—such as his imitation of Euripides, where he accounts for the relation of the lower gods to the higher ones on the basis of ancient lore—indicate his belief in polytheism. Over and above all the gods, he says, "reigns one who is supreme among men and gods. . . . This godhead is all eyes, all mind, all ears. . . . Without effort he controls everything by the power of his mind."

Through such writings as these, compounded partly of faith, partly of superstition, Xenophanes laid the foundation for a religious philosophy which had become so powerful a growth, after its cultivation by Aristotle, that it killed every thought planted in its shadow.

In the nontheologic branches of philosophy, Xenophanes speculated about many things. He declared that earth and water were the primary substances of the semi-infinite world, and that the earth moved downward into infinity, while the air moved in the opposite direction.

PARMENIDES

Parmenides is generally considered a disciple of Xenophanes, since he came from Elea in lower Italy, where Xenophanes held sway. He was in contact with the Pythagoreans of the time, and enjoyed the godlike adoration of his contemporaries. His high-flown philosophic teachings, which bear the customary title, *De Natura (On Nature)*, were highly revered by the ancients. The first part of this work is a compendium of playful variations on the sentence: "Existence is; nonexistence is not and cannot be conceived." This existence is conceived as invisible, immobile, boundless, and equally extended in all directions from the center. On this assumption, every thought which deals with motion and with the multifariousness of things must be contrary to existence and therefore false. It is obvious that such a concept discredits all natural sciences and their methods. And indeed Parmenides introduces the second part of his work, the so-called natural science section, with the words: "From now on learn to know the false ideas of man that you may understand the treacherous plan of my poem."

Certainly the confusion which reigns in his physics justifies this introduction. Here the world is divided into two hostile substances, light and darkness. These are thoroughly intermingled and held together by spheres composed of a similar mixture. Man partakes of the same mixture, and by the light within him he is able to see light, while by the darkness he recognizes darkness. The dead too possess the power of sensation, but they can sense only the dark. The control of all these mixtures lies in the hands of a demon.

We need not comment further upon the spirit which emanates from Parmenides' physics, but we should note

7

that the philosophic pride of the first metaphysicians and their disdain for scientific method laid down the path for all later Greek spiritual development.

ZENO OF ELEA

In his effort to prove the Parmenidean philosophy of a fundamental unity in the universe, Zeno of Elea (*ca.* 490-430 B.C.) succeeded in discrediting rather than strengthening his master's theory. Zeno tried to prove the impossibility of motion by innumerable dialectics. For example: "The moving arrow is at rest." This must be so because at every instant it is at one point and not at any other point, so that it rests during every instant; which means, in turn, that it rests during the sum of its instants—i.e., during all the time of its motion. Or: "Achilles could not catch up with the tortoise if it had the slightest advantage of him." For when Achilles reaches the tortoise's first point of rest, A, the tortoise has already moved to point B; and when he reaches B, it will have gone to C, and so on, infinitely. Again: "There is no motion." For in order for a body to move through space, one-half of it must first move through that distance. But this is impossible, since half of this half must move first, and then half of that half, and so on, to infinity. Therefore, all bodies are unmovable!

Here is one of the proofs which Zeno brought against the multiplicity and finiteness of that which exists (here he unknowingly contradicted his master) : The assumption of multiplicity in existence leads to contradictions which point, in one direction, to the nonspatiality, and in another, to the infinity, of objects. (1) To nonspatiality because the multiplicity of objects can be comprehended only through unity. But unity must be indivisible; therefore, no separate part of it can have extension. Accordingly, then, no object can have extension; i.e., it must be nonspatial. (2) On the other hand, every object must be infinite. For without size, no object can be considered as existent. But if it has size,

8

it consists of parts each one of which must also have size, and these parts in turn have other parts, and so on to infinity. Therefore, everything consists of an endless series of parts. In other words, it is endlessly large or infinite.

This method of reasoning led Aristotle to call Zeno the inventor of dialectics.

With their denial of the reality of motion in nature, the Eleatic philosophers discarded the whole visible world of movable things. Accepting the abstract reality of an everlasting, immobile, round-shaped being, which Parmenides had declared to be infinite, to them the whole world of living reality became no more than a phantom universe, "a non-existence seemingly existing." Thus Parmenides lent momentum to that tragicomic theory of mind substance which controlled the idealistic tendency in philosophy all the way down to the twentieth century. But what is forgivable in the unlearned Greek philosophers, and comprehensible in the superstition-ridden authors of ancient religious philosophy becomes unpardonable and incomprehensible in the mouths of the so-called scientific philosophers of the modern era. For these men (such as Kant) lived in an age of the healthy growth of the empirical spirit; yet, their eyes focused on a vacuum, they shamelessly improvised variations on the old Greek metaphysical myths instead of facing nature and its works, as all must do in the final analysis, even those who prefer to dream their way through life.

EMPEDOCLES

"But I wander among you as an immortal god, not as a mortal. I am honored by all as a god—as is fit!—and they weave wreaths for my head. But why do I speak about it as if it were something unusual? I am much more than you, O mortals steeped in many evils!"

So boasted Empedocles (*ca.* 400 B.C.)—philosopher, miracle man, politician and wanderer—fully convinced of his superhuman knowledge and abilities. For a long time

9

people were seduced by his words, but they finally adopted a more critical attitude toward his teachings. Many legends have come down to us about his death. He is said, for instance, to have been killed by enraged farmers. But the best-known is the story of the discovery of his sandals near Mount Aetna, which was said to have ejected them when the great magician threw himself into its crater to learn the secrets of Vulcan.

Extant fragments of the writings of Empedocles indicate that he was influenced by Orphic-Pythagorean theology and Heraclitean physics.

To the three primary substances of Heraclitus—fire, earth and water—Empedocles added a fourth, air. "Hear ye," he boasts, "I want to make known to you the primary substances of which all visible things were born: earth, the sea rich in waves, the humid air, and the Titan, wind, who encircles the whole sphere." Love and strife keep the primary substances in continual motion, and by means of this constant change, each of the primary substances comes into power in turn. "Out of this matter came all there was, is, and will be: trees, men and women, beasts and birds, water-sustained fishes, and even the gods, long-lived and rich in honor." [7]

It was in this way that the world was created: Love burst into being amid the hatred-dividing substances, setting up a great whirling motion which immediately drew all substances into itself. Out of this mixture, air separated first and built the heavens; fire followed and took its place beneath the heavens. Then the remaining water was squeezed out of the earth, and thus the gathering and division of the four substances was completed.

Living creatures grew slowly out of earth, at first only in masses of limbs. "Many heads without necks, naked arms without shoulders, eyes without foreheads wandered up and down. . . . Then many creatures grew up with double faces and double breasts; bodies, men in front and oxen in the back, grew up; still others with animal heads and the bodies of men." [8]

10

Among other curious beliefs held by Empedocles were these: That blood boiling about the heart gives us the power of thought. That the hair of the head is of the same substance as the feathers of birds and the leaves of trees. That girls are born when the male and female sperm fall upon cold ground; otherwise boys are born. From this it follows that men are darker, more courageous and fierier-tempered than women! [9] In the transmigration of souls, men who are reborn in the form of animals become lions living on mountaintops, while those who return as plants become laurel trees.[10]

These, and the rest of Empedocles' beliefs, are hardly subject to scientific proof. But his substance theory—the doctrine of the four elements—stubbornly dominated popular thinking till well into the eighteenth century, so great was the power and influence of the conservative tradition in philosophy.

ANAXAGORAS

Anaxagoras of Clazomenae (born *ca.* 500 B.C.) was still another of these early physicist-philosophers. At the age of twenty he went to Athens, where he became associated with Pericles. Anaxagoras also occupied himself with the study of elements. He believed that matter is made up of indestructible and invisible bodies which he named the "seeds" of matter. Among these, vapor and air are the most important.[11] Originally these seeds were mixed, until Reason called forth a whirling motion which separated the substances. Then darkness, cold and humidity gathered at the place where the earth is now, and the thin, warm and dry elements drew up into the ether. Water was the first element to separate out of the clouds; then out of the water came earth; and out of the earth, under the influence of cold, developed stones. After this separation of the substances, the activity of reason came to an end. This reason is entirely substantive: "It has complete supervision over everything,

11

and the greatest power," yet it is still only the "thinnest and purest of all substances."

Probably Diogenes of Apollonia, who identified Anaxagoras' "reason" with air, had the most nearly correct understanding of it. Here again, as with Anaxagoras, learned historians of philosophy have misinterpreted a physico-chemical thesis in terms of allegorical symbolism, and exploited it to a point where it can scarcely be recognized.

LEUCIPPUS

The natural sciences of the Greeks were brought to their highest point of abstraction by Leucippus, who lived in the days of Empedocles and Anaxagoras.

According to Leucippus, the matter of all objects is formed out of the "full" and the "empty." The "full" is divided into innumerable little particles which are so separated from each other by the "empty" that they have nothing empty remaining within them—for which reason they are called "atoms." These atoms are indestructible and uncreated, though differing in shape and form. They are impervious to any change except that of place.

In keeping with the theory of the "empty" and the "full," a body is heavier the more atoms it contains, and lighter the more empty space it holds. Not only weight and lightness, but hardness and softness, and the touch, smell and taste of a substance depend on its atomic formation. All coming into being and all destruction are merely changes in the relative arrangement of the atoms, or the mixture of the "full" and the "empty."

Very little is known about the father of the atomic theory. Theophrastus said he was a pupil of Parmenides; but we must wonder greatly at such a pupil of such a master!

Leucippus' major work, *The Great Order of the Universe,* was later ascribed to Democritus, his most distinguished pupil, an error seized upon by Epicurus in his effort to disprove the existence of Leucippus.[13]

In spite of its primitive aspects, the philosophy of Leucippus makes a definite break with the world theories of his contemporaries. His attempt to create a purely mechanistic theory of nature is quite worthy of note.

DEMOCRITUS

Democritus of Abdera (*ca.* 420-360 B.C.) gained fame for himself by championing the philosophy of Leucippus. Unfortunately, he clouded his master's simple nature philosophy with metaphysical problems. He scattered remarks on the creation of the world, on the soul (that it is composed of round, flat atoms, each of which separates into two body atoms), on demons (that they supersede man in size and longevity), on the effect of the evil eye, and so on, contributed greatly to the separation of later atomic studies from the early theories.

A widely traveled and learned man, Democritus, called "the Laughing Philosopher," left his contemporaries a compilation of sage rules for the conduct of life. Later teachers of ethics made good use of this work, so simple in form, so rich in content. But alas, these expounders of metaphysical morality so elaborated the natural and simple demands of daily life, that any hope of a practical ethics of daily conduct was buried beneath their huge, baseless, *ex-cathedra* structures of philosophic morality.

One cannot say that Democritus was the father of ethics. Superficially, this would seem to be the case. But our knowledge of Greek philosophy is limited: the ancients wrote very little, and of the little they wrote, only fragments have been preserved for us, and these not always of their most significant works.

PYTHAGORAS

At about the end of the sixth century B.C., a great religious movement invaded the cultural life of Greece. It was brought to birth by Pythagoras of Samos, who had left his homeland to travel in the neighboring Egyptian and other Middle Eastern countries. There he became acquainted with strange mathematical, astronomical and religious teachings, which he brought back with him to Crotona, in lower Italy. In the religious-philosophic sect which he organized, certain rites and laws of conduct are traceable to these Egyptian, Palestinian and Babylonian sources. Fantastic combinations of mathematics and astronomy with religious and moral principles laid the foundation of an ascetic order and a utopian communal life, which reached its climax in mystic orgies.

The Pythagorean society soon accumulated political power among the aristocracy, which led to growing friction with the people's parties and eventually to the persecution of the order. Fleeing adherents of the Pythagorean sect carried their beliefs throughout Greece.

From a scientific viewpoint, the teachings of Pythagoras have little validity, though some of his followers did pursue scientific studies. It is these which are generally identified with the Pythagorean philosophy.

THE PYTHAGOREANS

"What are things?" the Pythagoreans ask. And they answer: "Things are numbers." But since they find that the same phenomenon is repeated in many things, they continue: "Numbers are not things in themselves, but models in imitation of which things are made." "One" is the beginning of all things.[14] "Ten" is the all-controlling leader of godly and human lives.[15] Odd numbers are more perfect than even ones; they are better and more worthy. They are

14

identical with the "finite," while evil even numbers are identical with the infinite. One Pythagorean says that God is number seven; [16] another that reason is seven. The number of the soul is six, that of the body four. Here is the famous Pythagorean table of opposite pairs:

Finite	Infinite	Even	Odd
One	Many	Right	Left
Male	Female	Rest	Motion
Straight	Slanting	Light	Darkness
Good	Evil	Square	Right Angle

The world came into being by attracting to itself two and absorbing the two into one.[17] In the center of the earthly sphere is a fire which encircles the ten divine spheres. Nine of these spheres are those of the planets that were then known, but to bring the total up to the holy number, ten, another called the counter-earth was invented. These ten planets are framed in a glasslike hoop and revolve in unison about the flaming central fire.

On the passing of the "great year," creation repeats itself in every detail, including all personalities, experiences and events.[18]

Many Pythagoreans attempted to combine these and other teachings with the Eleatic, Heraclitean and atomic systems of thought, but they were not notably successful.

Belief in the transmigration of souls was widespread among the Pythagoreans; they considered not only animals and plants, but even sun dust particles to be wandering souls.[19]

The wide popularity of the Pythagorean games with numbers shows the power of confusion in mystic terminology under the appropriate circumstances. Plato, in his later years, was attracted by the obscurities of Pythagoras.

THE SOPHISTS

Around the second half of the fifth century B.C., the cultural status of Greece reached a high level, partly through the influence of Asiatic culture. At this time individual sciences began to develop and to seek theoretic expansion. Handbooks for various skilled occupations and arts had come into circulation, and scholars were making an effort to bring order into this new mass of knowledge. Numerous schools sprang up, most of which were conducted in the traditional methods of philosophy and rhetoric, though some pedagogues courageously resisted the inherited dogmas and techniques. Like other teachers, these nonconformists were called sophists, i.e., "learned sages." Only the Platonists applied this name to the more radical of them and linked the concept of sophism with that of destruction, quibbling and intellectual dishonesty.

The Sophists took as the foundation of their thought the division between nature and custom. The corollary division of rights into natural and statutory, which aimed at equal rights for all, must have been very humiliating to the aristocratic classes of Greece, with their philosophical systems of ethics.

"The creator made all people free; Nature made no slaves," taught Aleidamas, the Sophist.[20] And Hippias said, "I believe we are all of the same source, companions and citizens of nature, but the laws enslave many people contrary to the laws of nature." [21]

Amazed, Aristotle spoke out strongly against these rash Sophists who dared consider slavery the unnatural and evil act of the ruling aristocracy. After all, he (like his master Plato before him) had labored hard to prove conclusively the justice and necessity of slavery. "Others, on the contrary," Aristotle said, "think that the power of the master over his slave is unnatural; according to them, the difference between the free man and the slave exists only because of the laws, for men are not different by nature and slavery is practiced by force, not by right." [22]

16

Basing their arguments upon the fundamental materialism of nature and law, the Sophists demanded not only the liberation of the slaves, but equality of possession and education.[23] Aristotle and Plato, who had excluded artisans, laborers and farmers from both education and government, must have considered such demands the quibbling of fools. While Plato philosophized about a divine republic and metaphysical justice in a state that condoned human slavery and inequality, the Sophist Protagoras taught: "Man is the sum of all things. I can know nothing of the gods, whether they exist or not." The writings of the former burden-carrier were burned, and he himself had to flee for his life.

The Sophists by and large excelled in their sharp deviation from philosophic ideology which they considered useless play, and in the use of biting sarcasm to make it a laughingstock. There were among them, to be sure, some who were insincere and unreliable.

SOCRATES

Anyone wandering the streets of Athens around the year 400 B.C. might have run into a squat little man who harangued young and old in the market place. Everyone in Athens was familiar with this ill-shaped person; even the poets put him on the stage in their plays.

This man was Socrates, son of the stonecutter Sophroniscus and the midwife Phainarete. By trade he too was a stonecutter, but he did not follow his trade, a fact which brought him a goodly amount of abuse—and sometimes more than that—from his faithful wife, Xanthippe.

With all his eccentricities—he went barefoot in severest winter, conducted himself singularly, and tried to plumb the very depths of a man's mind with his endless questioning—Socrates was an intensely altruistic man, inspired by a fanatic love of the truth. His pupils considered him to be the best and wisest of men. Xenophon said of him: "Socrates was so pious that he undertook nothing without the

17

will of the gods; so just that he did not one injustice—more than that, he was kind to everyone who came in contact with him. He was so much the master of himself that he never preferred what was merely pleasurable to what was good; and so virtuous that he never made a mistake in the choice between the good, the better and the worse—in a word, he was the best and happiest of mankind."

To test the truth of an oracle which declared him the wisest man in Athens, Socrates went from man to man to see if he could find out whether he really was wiser than all others. And behold! he found that all who were superior to him in one respect, in one art or another, fooled themselves into thinking that they were superior in every way. "I, on the other hand," he said, "knowing my ignorance, do not fool myself into believing that I know anything." [24]

The fact is that Socrates wanted to teach his fellow men, with all the persuasive and critical powers at his command, to look for something better in their private as well as their public lives. The goal he pursued was moral progress, the betterment of private conduct as well as improvement of the state. He demanded justice of the state and moderation in personal life, demands which in old Athens were bound, sooner or later, to bring about his downfall. Embittered opponents of his courageous teachings succeeded finally in bringing the sage before the tribunal and pushing through his conviction on charges of blasphemy and corruption of youth.

After his execution, the conscience of the Greeks was sorely troubled, but many Greeks were yet to be sacrificed to political and social intolerance.

Socrates' disciple, the poet-philosopher Plato, made Socrates the exponent of his own thoughts in his writings, and thus involved the older man in metaphysical speculations of his own invention. Aristotle, in turn, working with the poetic image of Plato-Socrates before his eyes, named the great skeptic the founder of logic and the discoverer of the inductive method of thought and of definition in general.[25] These assumptions he based entirely upon the construction of the Platonic dialogues in which Socrates plays the leading role.

THE SOCRATICS

Many thinkers besides Plato made Socrates the ideal philosopher of their systems, always, of course, investing his image with their own ideas. The central idea in these philosophies is generally the notion of virtue for which its champion, Socrates, sacrificed his life.

ANTISTHENES, the founder of an ascetic movement, declared that virtue can be acquired, not through wisdom and study, but only by a denial of life. The statement, "Rather be insane than pleased," originated with him. His followers lived with communally possessed wives and, because of this and their physical shamelessness, which they considered a higher form of the philosophic life, they were called Cynics ("dogs").

DIOGENES OF SINOPE, a pupil of Antisthenes, is known, because of his exaggerated emphasis on abstinence, as "the mad Socrates." A barrel served the naked Diogenes as a home, and a wooden vessel as a drinking cup.[26] Once witnessing a boy draw drinking water with his bare hands, Diogenes threw down his cup and turned away in shame: the boy had outdone him in deriving contentment from nothing.

The schools of begging philosophers disbanded with the rise of the Stoics, less than a century later, only to return to fashion in the days of the Roman Caesars.

ARISTIPPUS OF CYRENE, the apostle of hedonism, stood in direct contrast to Antisthenes. His philosophy is summed up in the words: "Whatever brings pleasure is good, what brings pain is evil; all else is indifferent." He considered the sciences unnecessary, useless and pointless. Of the disciples of Aristippus, some expressed a preference for bodily pleasures, others for spiritual ones.

There was also an indifferentist among them, HE-

GESIAS, whom they called Peisistanatos ("the convert of suicide"). His philosophy declared the highest good to be a state of painlessness, and since that is rarely attainable, this ancient Schopenhauer expressed a preference for death to life. In Egypt his lectures had to be prohibited because so many of his listeners committed suicide.

A group more interested in dialectics gathered around EUCLID OF MEGARA, who wove complicated logical tangles out of the threads of Parmenidean physics and Socratic ethics. For a time Plato was in close touch with this group. A whole series of his dialogues (*Theaetetus, Parmenides, Sophistos*) are a product of this dialectic. EUBULIDES, a pupil of Euclid, excelled in composing summary sentences that reflect the character of this school. One of his best-known begins: "How many hairs must one lose to become bald-headed?" [27] Another runs: "What you did not lose you still have; you did not lose your horns; therefore you have horns."

PLATO

Aristocles, later called Plato ("The Broad"), was born in Athens in the year 427 B.C., the scion of an old aristocratic family. In early youth he occupied himself with the composition of poetry which, after his meeting with Socrates, took ethical and social problems as its theme. After Socrates' death, however, he came under the influence of other thinkers—Euclid for one. Then, while traveling in lower Italy he came in contact with the Pythagorean school, which left its mark on his thought.

Plato's interest in politics led to his indulging in numerous reform experiments, most of which proved highly unfortunate. After trying his hand at teaching, he finally in 387 B.C. opened a school of philosophy in the gymnasium of the academy at Athens. With few interruptions, he continued as a teacher until his death in 347.

Many of his works have come down to us. The genuineness of some of those attributed to him is highly dubious, but the authenticity of the major ones is beyond question. The letters and definitions which have been handed down over his name are doubtless forgeries.

Plato did not express the whole of his philosophic viewpoint in a single work—insofar as he can be said to have a specific viewpoint, considering his ambiguous method of expression. Starting always from a fresh point of departure, he examined many ideas in turn, so that virtually all his works come to an end without stating a positive conclusion.

His physics and astronomy are rooted in Pythagorean axioms and hardly rise above the level of any representative of the Pythagorean school. Plato's interest lies in his political philosophy and ethics, although here too he shows the marked influence of the aristocratic Pythagoreans, so that it might be more accurate to call him a Pythagorean than a Socratic. Thus he advises barring all farmers, artisans and businessmen from political and cultural pursuits.[28] All higher public functions, including the advantages rising from political power, should be the exclusive province of the aristocrats, whom he considers naturally ordained for higher callings. With a narrow-mindedness that seems especially curious in his day and environment, he goes so far as to attribute to the aristocrat the natural heritage of a philosophic mind.[29] To the warrior class, which he values above the working people, he gives special privileges for the sake of the nobility's safety and welfare.

And this "divine" state, this chimera of an aristocratic salon philosopher, sets up as its goal the realization of virtue! Whether Plato calls it "real knowledge," "happiness," "contentment" or "justice" (the subtitle of his *Republic*), it is certainly not the virtue of which the hemlock-poisoned sage was speaking when he said that it is better to suffer injustice than to commit it. How can there be "virtue" where arrogance has grown to the point of mania? And can he be teaching justice who dedicates his mind entirely to the privileged classes? To uphold the aris-

21

tocrat's idleness and right of possession, to deprive the working masses of every possibility of advancement, to establish the warrior class securely between these two—this is the avowed aim of Plato's political planning. His philosophy accepts the enslavement of the common people as natural, and considers their education, enlightenment and acquisition of equal rights nothing less than sinful. And all this at a time when the voices of the Sophists were calling, throughout the Greek state, for the liberation of the people!

How singular are the internal arrangements of Plato's philosophic state! Here, for instance, at a certain appointed time, the philosophically gifted statesmen, led by the magistracy, are to be turned loose among the women. Distinction in war implies precedence here too. After drawing lots and casting dice, the human herd is brought to the waiting women, and in religious (*sic!*) ceremony, all are ushered into the bedroom. After the act, the women return to their daily work, the warriors to the parade, the philosophers and aristocrats to their meditations on virtue. The working people, naturally, are excluded from this, as from all other, holidays.

The children, who never come to know either father or mother, are brought immediately after birth into a general nursery, where they are nursed promiscuously by the women—when the latter are not occupied with the men in gymnastics and music (these being the only fit occupations for aristocrats).

Since the children are taken from their mothers immediately after birth, and a mother could hardly be expected to name the men who were given to her during the sex-banquet, incest enters boldly through door and window. What is to prevent the coupling of parents and children, and of brothers and sisters at the Platonic feast?

It is noteworthy that Plato recommended philosophers as the kings of this state, which he thought would be viewed with great favor by the gods—a not insignificant demand.[30]

In addition to his "best state," Plato proposed another which he called the "second-best" state, somewhat more moderate in its customs, but hardly less confused. Kant's remark that the Platonic state was the greatest achievement of human liberty is typical of the reactionary trend of the modern philosopher.

Of what, then, does Platonic philosophy consist? Here again there is a dearth of concreteness. Our philosopher fancies that God formed as many souls as there are fixed stars and placed each soul upon a star where it might contemplate eternal Ideas. Later, the Creator planted these souls on earth, where they were dressed in the "lower soul's parts" and the body. Thus man consists of three parts: mind, courage and desire.

After death, all souls come to judgment; and evil ones are cast into hell, while good souls fly up to Heaven where they remain until the arrival of the next millennium. After rebirth, each soul has the right to select a new form of life. Naturally, those that have been incarnated in the bodies of beasts may now turn human again. This process of reincarnation is repeated ten times until "the great year" passes; then all souls return to Heaven, whereupon the cycle begins anew.

Plato's physics, even more than his eschatology, betrays the Pythagorean influence, as Timon of Philius (ca. 300 B.C.) charged. The Platonic method of exposition, however, which must seek its equal in mystification, justifies a certain claim to originality.

The Pythagoreans taught: "Beyond this world of decline and motion, rests the eternal being of number. Number is the essential being; it is the form after which things were modeled. Number is itself 'by virtue of itself'; it is uncreated and indestructible; it is creative and the cause of all visible things."

Plato the poet lifted numbers out of the dream world of the Pythagoreans and put "Ideas" in their place. The form was new, but the mysteries remained the same: "Beyond this world of decay and motion, the eternal being of the Idea rests. The Idea is the essential being, it is the form upon which things were modeled. The Idea is itself 'by

23

virtue of itself"; it is uncreated and indestructible; it is creative and the cause of all things."

In his later years, Plato made his metaphysical leanings clearer by becoming a complete Pythagorean and putting the "Ideas" of his philosophy on the same level with Pythagorean numbers.[31] By this he improved the consistency, but hardly the essence, of his theories. Plato wound up, finally, in a species of religious superstition. He located his "Ideas" somewhere above the world (*hyper uranios*), in the place where God created matter.[32] The fact that Plato called this God the "form of the good" (he called Him some other names as well!) opened the door to the subsequent endless allegorization of his philosophy. It was not long before some religions, desperate for philosophic underpinnings, began to bolster themselves with his concept of an elastic God. Because of this concept, any spiritual movement could claim Plato as its own. Even Utilitarianism and Communism have appropriated him as godfather.

The philosophic dream castles of Plato, created by a metaphysical aestheticism and decorated with fanciful moral ornaments, rest on a foundation of transcendental ideas. No matter how beguilingly Plato the poet sings in praise of the noble Socrates, the melody of his devotion to beauty is marred by incoherence.

THE PLATONISTS

The school which Plato founded was continued by his disciples for literally hundreds of years. His immediate followers, SPEUSIPPUS and XENOCRATES, emphasized even more frankly the Pythagorean content of his philosophy, though they continued to hold the academy in Plato's name. Xenocrates thought it right to identify God with the number "one," the other numbers being used for other concepts.[33]

Only ARCESILAUS and CARNEADES OF CYRENE were able to bring some clarification into the Platonic-

Pythagorean schools. But academic dogmatism remained dominant until it was swallowed up in the shallow eclecticism which became the trade-mark of Platonism for hundreds of years. Meanwhile, Aristotle of Stagira, a pupil of Plato, developed his own school of philosophy independent of the academicians.

ARISTOTLE

Aristotle of Stagira, later called "the Stagirite," was born in 384 B.C., the year of Demosthenes' birth. During his lifetime the Greeks waged their tragic struggle for freedom against the robber king, Philip of Macedonia. Aristotle enjoyed the special favor of Philip and was appointed tutor to his son Alexander, that same Alexander who died in distant Asia at the age of thirty-three, after a life crowded with plunder, pillage and excess. Upon the death of Alexander, whom a glory-blinded generation named "the Great," Aristotle was put on trial by the Greeks because of his friendship with the tyrant and his henchman-ruler Antipater, and was driven from the country.

For nearly twenty years Aristotle belonged to the Platonic school, without, however, being able to get a teaching position in it. When he conducted a sharp, hardly justified polemic against his master, Plato compared him with a filly that kicks the dam whose milk it drank. It was said that on one occasion, when Plato's favorite pupils were absent, Aristotle argued so ruthlessly with the eighty-year-old master that Plato was obliged to remain away from the academy for three months.

The writings of Aristotle, of which we have many fragments as well as complete works, represent for the most part lectures delivered to his students at the lyceum. Aristotle was an eclectic by temperament and had little to offer that was genuinely new. As in the case of Plato, his physics, compared with the physics of the so-called natural philosophers, shows a regression rather than an advance. On the other hand, his encyclopedias afford an excellent picture of the level of learning in his day.

His scientific treatises are generally geared to the primitive thought processes of the man in the street. Thus, in discussing fowls, he lumps birds and insects in a single category; or he explains that a seed contains the most digestible food and is a foam composed of air and water; [34] or that if animals face north at the instant of conception, they will bring forth females, while if they face south the progeny will be male.[35]

And this is the nature study that, under the shadow of religious dogmatism, provided the basis for all scientific works well into the seventeenth century! (*Cf.* Rondelet, Gesner, Johnston, Lister, Aldrovandi.) For almost two thousand years science was dominated by Aristotelianism.

Following the prevalent custom, Aristotle devoted a great part of his works to dialectics, in which he laid particular stress on the forms of judgment. His exhaustive speculations on judgments and predictions (which Kant claimed make up a complete formal logic) were, until very recently, a main subject of higher education, despite the fact that they possessed little value in themselves, and were so complicated by nonessentials as to be difficult to comprehend.

But "logic" has always been an attractive exercise of man's mind, and we shall see later how many things Kant and other logicians "proved" by its ingenious manipulation.

Like Plato, Aristotle was convinced of the existence of transcendent beings and powers. Contrary to Plato, however—who called every mind-transcending element an "Idea" (later, a number)—Aristotle called the creative substance "form." Form, then, assumed all those attributes which since the days of Parmenides had been ascribed to primary substances. Opposition to this form is the only possible attribute of all the "unreal" material substances which the form strives to bind, and is therefore the cause of all imperfections, limitations and meanness. God is nothing except absolute form, and he brings forth nothing evil. In the words of Plato, "God is ever and in every way good." [36]

Although matter is unreal, according to Aristotle, it is in constant motion "by virtue of its potentialities." Who, then, is the motivator? he asks, and answers: God is the prime mover, the absolute; God is the form, the form without matter. God is also the aim and goal of the world. Yes, a thing is perfect or imperfect according to its distance from God. Nearest God is the fixed star-heaven, the empyrean, which He touches, *not being touched by it in return.*

The universe in its entirety is finite and is divided into a supernal world of stars and the world of earth. The starry world is filled with eternal ether, which moves in a spheric orbit and is the essence of the star system. The fixed stars are likewise composed of ether and are located in a hollow sphere, with which they revolve around the earth. Several spheres revolve about each planet, of which there are fifty-five. These are kept in constant motion by the external force of God and the internal drive of the sphere spirits.

Like Plato, Aristotle viewed ethics as a political matter. The individual can attain perfection only within the state. Outside the state man is either a beast or a god. The state was created before man, directly from nature, and not according to human plan or arrangement. That the whole precedes its parts is a metaphysical rule; therefore the state preceded the individual.[37]

Without concerning himself too much with this prehuman state, Aristotle hastens to a consideration of justice, the major virtue. Having defined the essence of justice as the proper division of social advantages and disadvantages, he proceeds to elaborate his best of all possible states. Like Plato, he gives his ideal society the form of a Greek city-state, for he thought only the Hellenes were able to create an adequate civic organization. Aristotle also separates the wealthy classes, whom he considers natural rulers, from the working people, with the consequence that all manual labor is imposed on the nonpropertied classes. Considering the poorer classes less worthy of concern than the well-fed, property-owning aristocrats, he argues zealously to prove that their unprivileged position has been ordained by God

27

and Nature. He compares the workman who has nothing to offer but his body, to an animal; and since his function differs little from that of a domestic beast, both laborers and animals should supply philosophers and statesmen with a livelihood.[38]

Of those whose only possession is themselves, he says that "it is right and useful that they should be slaves." This philosopher who, thanks to the beneficence of the Macedonian tyrants, could live in the greatest luxury, naturally has nothing but insult and contempt for the liberal Sophists' demand for freedom and equality.

But how democratic is a philosophy that states: "The laborer is a living chattel and is not only the slave of his lord, but belongs to him completely"?[39] Of what point is the meticulous discussion of division of rights, the practice of moderation, the cultivation of ethical conduct, in such a situation? To us this has the hollow ring of philosophy set in a moral vacuum. It is apparent that Aristotelian political philosophy and state ethics could easily become the grounds of support for many later tyrannical institutions.

Not even virtue is within the poor man's reach, for to become virtuous one must possess a strong will, and this Aristotle denies the poor man with the same compelling logic that he uses to attribute it to the aristocrat. Only one virtue is permitted the poor man, the virtue of obedience to his aristocratic master; *that* he can bring to a certain state of perfection![40]

Matters are of course far different with the rich.[41] Side by side with the pursuit of the great practical virtue, the golden mean, Aristotle praises the virtue of a life dedicated to wisdom. We have already had more than a hint as to what such a virtue, and such a life, had to offer. The acme of virtue, however, is attainable only within the state, since the highest of all goods is justice.

As a psychologist, Aristotle shows his familiarity with Plato's threefold division of the soul. The indestructible "by-soul" whose function is as incomprehensible as its relation to the "main soul," was one of Plato's ideas (*Cf.*

Phaidon). Aristotle reiterates that the existence of the mortal "main soul" is dependent on the unsuffering and immortal "by-soul." [42] Just as the "by-soul" enters the body of man from the outside as a spark from God, so it is not destroyed at death. This division of the soul into a mortal and immortal part (the *"spiritus"* and *"animus"* of the Middle Ages and Renaissance) long remained a favorite theme in philosophy. The charm of an invisible "something" coming into man's life out of nowhere exerted a peculiar and understandable power of attraction on the speculative philosophic mind. It was only empirical psychology which eventually put an end to this fairyland of the soul.

Aristotle was also the author of several essays on poetry. Although he did not demand scientific truth from poetry, he placed it above history because history gives only the truth of single events, while poetry presents universal ideas.[43]

THE ARISTOTELIANS

The so-called peripatetic school of Aristotle took much the same course as the school of Plato. In their works the followers of Aristotle limited themselves to the completion and elaboration of their master's teachings. Their preoccupation with the writing of history always gave them a certain superiority over the Platonists. Among Aristotle's immediate followers, STRATON OF LAMPSACUS (*ca.* 280 B.C.) achieved some originality by returning to the old Ionic physics. In later centuries we find the peripatetic school producing nothing but commentaries on Aristotle, until it finally lost itself in Neoplatonism.

In the physics of Leucippus, the Greek natural sciences had reached their peak. In comparison, the metaphysics of Plato and Aristotle were a regression. Plato did little for the development of empiric science; Aristotle was an eclectic. What they taught was old; what they innovated was imperfect. How meager is their true knowledge in comparison with their heaven-storming metaphysics! With what bold daring did they tackle the task of explaining the planets, without being able to evaluate sensibly the smallest event on earth! What a barren physics this is, erected on the shaky ground of transcendentalism; what an empty astronomy, based on theological superstitution; what a sterile natural science, achieved through metaphysical speculation instead of through the healthy observation of nature; and what a dangerous political philosophy and debased state morality!

Yet when every criticism has been leveled at them, Plato and Aristotle remain the indisputable founders of what is called Western philosophy. To this day they have not been superseded. Even such contemporary philosophers as Scheler, Bergson, Whitehead, and Husserl have revived the dream-world spirit of these ancient metaphysicians. In the course of this book we shall see how little has been added to popular Western philosophy—save by way of Christian mythology—since the days of Aristotle. Later philosophers tend simply to elaborate on the threadbare motifs of the ancients. Christian theology attached itself to the old Greek speculations and from this union sprang a thousand-and-one-year-old phantastically arranged web of metaphysics culminating in Thomas Aquinas and Albertus Magnus.

THE STOICS AND EPICUREANS

In its early phases, philosophy, as the study of the transcendent, had searched for a method of investigation to reach out into areas where the mind of the scientist refused to work. Now, with the Aristotelian and Platonic schools, it entered a new stage. For the immediate future, the old, rather vague concept of "a thirst for knowledge" was narrowed down to specific moral-religious speculations. The schools of Zeno and Epicurus, which dominated the cultural life of Greece and Italy until they were replaced by Christian dogmatism, were typical of this period.

The dictum of EPICURUS (341-270 B.C.), "Philosophy is the art of reaching a happy life by means of research," [44] and the definition of the Stoic SENECA (4 B.C.-65 A.D.), "Philosophy is the science of moral conduct and the study of how to act properly," [45] are typical utterances of this "moral" epoch of philosophy. Seen in their true light, Stoicism and Epicureanism appear as only slightly differentiated continuations of the philosophies of an Antisthenes and an Aristippus. Socrates was idealized by both schools.

The revival of the philosophy of the Cynics came about, as previously noted, through the Stoic teachings of the Phoenician merchant Zeno, who was driven into the consoling arms of philosophy by the loss of his entire wealth in a shipwreck. After many years of wandering through the Greek schools, he founded a school of his own. But the academician Polemon accused him of a total lack of original ideas: "You are caught, Zeno, as you sneak in through the back door, turning the old ideas around and dressing them in Phoenician clothing." [46]

The teachings of Zeno deviate but slightly from those of the Cynics. Asceticism and an unshakable faith in the judgments and preordinations of the gods remained the leading principles of Stoicism. Natural science was completely neglected, and in its neglect the Stoics exhibited a certain pride (not unlike that shown by the followers of the French metaphysician Bergson in our own time). Even logic was valued only insofar as it contributed to a happy existence. Ariston, a pupil of Zeno, observed laconically: "Logic does not concern us, and physics is beyond our ken." [47]

Such natural science as may be found among the Stoics is borrowed from either Heraclitus or later thinkers. Their philosophy is almost exclusively a study in values. Its aim and goal is a state of calm and indifference, which can be attained by various methods. It should be seen immediately, argue the Stoics, that the greatest happiness, human and divine, lies in the immobility of the soul. Those who would live through the flux of things, advises Zeno, should live "in complete harmony with nature." [48] In ardent language, he praises the philosophic man, who desires nothing, hopes for nothing, fears nothing, strives against no one, loves no human being. The Stoics knew no middle road: either a man is a philosopher, a sage, or he is a fool. All emotions are a disease of the soul, and the sole duty of philosophy is to cure it. The highest wisdom consists in the subjugation of the emotional life; emotions not only toward things, but also toward people. Love of father or mother, wife or child must be rooted out if philosophic peace is to be obtained. "If you caress your child or wife," the famous Stoic EPICTETUS (*ca.* 50 A.D.) said, "say to yourself that it is not different than if you were caressing any person. Then, if he dies, you will be unaffected." [49]

Clearly, this is a somewhat limited philosophy, with a singular morality, aimed at the rather trivial goal of providing the beloved ego with the greatest possible number of pleasurable hours. According to this morality, the man who worries about no one, never feels sympathy for a fellow man, and is careful to avoid all discomfort while keeping his every desire satisfied, may be called a sage. But it remains more than a little doubtful whether the highest human good lies in this pedantic apology for selfishness!

Christian morality, also opposed to personal love and egotism, took many ideas from Stoicism. One of these is phrased: "Who does not hate father and mother for my sake is not worthy of me." This imitation of Stoicism went so far that, in the days of Julian, it was possible for a cleric to issue Epictetus' handbook of Stoic morals as a Christian text simply by substituting the name of Paul for that of Socrates!

Not only in morals, but in the field of theology, Christianity shows many resemblances to Stoicism. Hundreds of years before the birth of Christ, the Stoics preached doctrines remarkably Christian in tone.[50] The works of God are full of signs and premonitions, according to the stoic MARCUS AURELIUS.[51] Similarly, Seneca said that the gods have predestined the longevity and fate of every man.[52] The

32

Stoics were convinced, not only of divine predestination, but also of the truth of godly premonition. Zeno wrote a book on the theme, and CHRYSIPPUS, the pride of the Stoics, attempted to justify this superstition.

POSIDONIUS (*ca.* 50 B.C.), who with his teacher, PANAITIUS (*ca.* 120 B.C.), planted Stoicism in Italy, brought to Stoic philosophy a belief in dreams, soothsaying and ecstatic prophecy, and Western philosophy has been influenced by such beliefs ever since. Posidonius claimed considerable knowledge of the souls of the departed which float in the air. According to Seneca, the gods make known the future by means of lightning—not merely an occasional event, but the whole course of history.[53] While Marcus Aurelius was convinced of the assistance given man by the gods through oracles and revelatory dreams,[54] Epictetus was most serious about reading signs in the entrails of animals and in the flight of birds.[55] He was, indeed, called a "crypto-Christian." The consoling preachments of Seneca, that gods floating in the air would turn to the aid of mortals if beseeched in prayer,[56] brought about an exchange of letters between the Stoic philosopher and the Apostle Paul.

The life of Seneca demonstrates how Stoicism was for many simply a matter of fashion. This man, who had fulsome praise for the life of asceticism and negation, left a fortune of 300 million sesterces, accumulated by graft and the theft of other people's inheritances. This same Seneca, who condemned participation in politics as unethical, was subservient to Nero and Agrippina in the execution of their bloody deeds, and even made a bawd of himself in order to retain the emperor's favor. Even in his servility he was faithless, for as he flattered the living Caesar devotedly, he mocked and besmirched the dead one.

The Stoics were divided in their opinions about life after death. While Cleanthes gave to all souls continued existence, Chrysippus offered immortality only to philosophers.[57] Seneca reported quite minutely on the happiness and suffering of the soul after death.[58]

Along with the fashionable philosophy of Stoic asceticism, the spreading philosophy of Epicurus held a special attraction for the pleasure-loving circles of Rome. EPICURUS OF SAMOS (341-270 B.C.) founded a philosophic or ethical society in Athens in the year 306, which for various reasons caught the fancy of many men and women. The aim of this school was less the study of the sciences, which were scorned as useless, than the pursuit of a merry life. There is extant an anthology of salacious anecdotes by Diogenes Laertius on the conduct of the school, which was well attended by prostitutes. Old reports made much of the revelry in the gardens of Epicurus, and Horatius Flaccus (65-88 A.D.), a later pupil of the school, described himself as "a swine from the herd of Epicurus." [59]

Starting with the hedonism of Aristippus, Epicurus gave his followers lessons in human desires and their fulfillment. "Desire marks the beginning and the end of life," he declared. At another point he said, "I do not know what to understand by the good other than the happiness of the table, of amorous desire, and such pleasures as come through the mediacy of the sense of hearing and of sight." [60] Then again: "Ethics and virtue and whatever else of their kind there may be should be recognized only insofar as they increase desire. Insofar as they do not do this we should let them pass."

So we see that Stoicism and Epicureanism, in spite of fundamentally opposing starting points, lead to the same ethical conclusion, namely, the setting up of extreme egotism and the satisfaction of desire as the highest good.

We have remarked that the philosophy of Epicurus was borrowed from earlier authors, Leucippus in particular. To this statement we must make the exception that his theory of the atomic composition of the soul is original. The gods too are composed of atoms, according to Epicurus, but of finer atoms existing in better worlds.[61] Still, that does not free them of natural desires; they are even more subject to these than man is! They converse, of course, in Greek. Epicurus placed little value on the influence of the gods upon human history, much to the sorrow of the pious

34

Seneca, who would have preferred to see divine predestination in every event.[62] But Epicurus knew real virtue when he saw it, and he allowed his gods to be real Epicureans, passing their hours in pleasure and blessed idleness.

THE SKEPTICS

By the opening of the Christian era, the fanciful metaphysical speculations of Plato and Aristotle had penetrated the cultural life of all the Greek and Roman countries. Every serious effort at empirical investigation had been pushed into the background by the dominant philosophy, and the thoughts of the youth had been shunted from the study of nature to the endless speculations of metaphysics. The word had carried off the victory over reality.

Toward the end of the fourth century B.C., PYRRHO, a pupil of the logician Stiplon, founded a school which had no other purpose than to teach the impossibility of knowledge. It is best, said Pyrrho, not to draw any conclusions from experience, i.e., not to form any opinions whatsoever. A contemporary of Cicero, AENESIDEMUS OF KNOSSOS, drew up articles of faith among which was this unshakable principle of refraining from judgment.

Carneades later carried the doctrine of suspension of judgment so far that a pupil had to admit that he could not tell toward which of two opposing principles his philosophy inclined. As late as the second century A.D., the skepticism of Pyrrho was represented by Sextus, who was called Empiricus. But neither skepticism nor the desire for knowledge had any effect on honest investigation. The skepticism of the ancients was rather a reaction against an unbounded metaphysical speculation which was willing to treat the most daring assumptions as absolutely certain facts. One need only remember the poverty of Greek and Roman intelligence, and recall the fifty-five philosophy-storming spheres of Aristotle, to appreciate the skepticism of the ancients. It was skepticism of the knowledge which metaphysics pretended to offer since real inquiry and genuine knowledge had been crowded out by the metaphysical method. Mystification had overgrown science and robbed it of every chance of development.

This was to remain the status quo for a long, long time, for at least the thousand years during which philosophy united with religion to see man through that darkness over Europe which our era had to call the Dark Ages.

PHILO JUDAEUS

Before the sky had cleared of its mist of old metaphysics, the clouds of mythology swept in from the East. This time Alexandria was the source of the phantasy. There it had its beginning, but not its end.

It was in Alexandria that Jewish and Greek dream worlds met and contracted that fateful kin-marriage between religion and philosophy. While the Jewish scholars in Palestine remained apart from Greek influence and dedicated themselves to the elaboration of the Torah, a group of Alexandrian Jews became sympathetically disposed to Greek wisdom and began to incorporate it into their own teachings. We must keep in mind that these men encountered Greek philosophy in the guise of Neopythagoreanism and Neoplatonism, in which forms it was comparatively easy for them to discover points of similarity to their religion. Some Jews, after contact with learned Greeks and Romans, made efforts to interpret their holy books in terms of pagan symbolism. They soon uncovered an inner kinship between pagan allegories and their own myths. Some Jews carried the identification so far as to declare that the wisdom of the philosophers must have been drawn from the Torah. The comment of Nemenius (ca. 150 B.C.) is typical: "What is Plato if not an ethical Moses?"

Philo Judaeus stood in the forefront of the Hellenizing Jews. He called philosophy the belief in divine revelation and Moses the mouthpiece of God.[63] Believing the Jews to

36

be God's chosen people, he considered them especially pre-destined to philosophy. Since the Greeks also showed a disposition to philosophy, Philo claimed that Pythagoras, like Plato and Aristotle, had drawn his ideas from the book of Moses.

The philosophic writings of Philo remind one strongly of the dialectics of the Scholastics. Generally starting with a passage from the Bible, he attaches to it the most daring philosophic allegories. For instance, in the story of the Creation, Adam represents Reason, introduced into Paradise to care for the trees, i.e., the virtues. He is misled by sensuality (Eve) to seek the reality of the outer world through the birth of Cain. The four rivers in Paradise stand for the four cardinal virtues.

Abraham, Isaac and Jacob represent to Philo the learned, natural and exercised virtues. Hagar, Abraham's slave wife, whom he drove out upon the instigation of Sarah, symbolizes perfect virtue. When Abraham answered the query of the three wanderers as to Sarah's whereabouts with the words, "She is in the hut," he was saying that virtue is in the soul. The three wanderers themselves were God and His two powers or attributes. The sacrifice of Isaac by Abraham means that the wise offer their children as a sacrifice to God, to whom alone happiness belongs— only sorrow and fear being the lot of man!

Whoever cares to dig into this amazing tangle should look into Philo's commentary, "On Abraham." Those on Isaac and Jacob have, alas, been lost.

Philo's interpretation of the life of Joseph is equally whimsical. He makes Pharaoh the symbol of an autocratically ruled state, while Potiphar represents the passions of the people. Joseph, on the other hand, is the sincere statesman who hates demagoguery and resists being swayed by the populace.

Philo accepts the Commandments as literally inspired by God.[64] One part of the Jewish law was given to the Jews by God Himself, orally or in writing, while for the other God used Moses as his mouthpiece.[65] Philo held on to the laws and customs of the Jews with orthodox firmness, and proclaimed that the universal spread of the faith would mean the redemption of all mankind. Nevertheless, Jewish authors of later ages tended to ignore Philo, because his fanciful philosophizing struck them as dangerous. In his comments on the universally accepted Decalogue, for instance, Philo interpolated remarks on the Pythagorean philosophy of numbers.

The Hellenism in Philo's philosophy remains, however, merely a foreign element, called into the service of the faith which is appropriate to religious teachings. A single sentence of the Torah must have appeared, in his eyes, more worthy than all the writings of the Greeks and Romans combined. Necessarily, therefore, Philo yielded to the Jewish prophets and patriarchs every claim of priority. The teachings of the philosophers concerning freedom must have been taken from the Torah, "for Moses has already told us how the foolish Esau was to serve the wise Jacob." [66] Yet Philo was so infatuated by Platonism that he converted the severe and angry God of the Hebrews into a Platonic, kindly controller of fate who would hurt no one. This metamorphosed Deity hesitates even to punish; punishment is delegated to his representatives playing the role of judges. For since the days of Plato, the kindly Lord (as Philo calls him) is the cause only of good, not of evil. Only man, who ungratefully commits sins instead of behaving virtuously, is evil. So kindly God, instead of destroying the evil brood which he has so generously created, lets them live on, punishing them only with hard labor.[67]

As for the genuinely Platonic in Philo: Man is a mediary being, a member of two worlds, the world of the senses and sin and the world of philosophic virtue. (Kant called them the visible world and the intelligible world.[68]) As soon as man understands his sinfulness, he must abase himself before God, i.e., he must believe in the infallibility of God's laws and deny his own self. If man will do this, the Holy Spirit (Logos), God's representative on earth, will grow compassionate and give the repentant sinner a chance to

38

do penance. But by believing in the Torah, man may become more like God and rid himself of the sensual world in order to enter the transcendent world. (*Cf.* Plato.) God permitted the chosen one in a moment of highest ecstasy to see His face.[69]

The function of God's representative, the Logos, is rather loosely defined. In general he plays merely the role of a mediator, a kind of interpreter between matter and God. It is noteworthy that Philo often refers to the Platonic Logos as "the only-begotten son of God." This is of the greatest importance in dealing with the Christian teachings about the Logos, for it is impossible to conceive of an exegesis of the Christian Logos theory without taking Philo's philosophy into account. Philo's interpretation of the Logos as a radiation or emanation of God was, like his concept of angels and demons, of decisive importance for Christian philosophy. However slight his influence on Jewish theology, his influence on Christian metaphysics cannot be overestimated. It was he who showed the first educated Christians the way to master the dominant Greek philosophy, without having to give up their belief in God, the only-begotten Son, and the Holy Logos. He was the model for the first Christian philosophers and the teacher of their successors.

With the orthodox Jew, Philo, who declared every letter of the Old Testament the revelation of God, and held a Mosaic interpretation of the redemption of the world, we have reached the threshold of the second epoch of European philosophy, generally designated as the Christian era.

JESUS OF NAZARETH

While Philo Judaeus was devoting himself to the interpretation of the Torah in Alexandria, a curious occurrence was taking place in near-by Canaan. A Jewish carpenter Yeshua ben Josef, called Jesus by the Greeks, suddenly emerged from obscurity and declared himself the long-awaited Messiah sent by God to the oppressed Jewish tribes. The kingdom of God had come with him, he declared, and before a generation had passed, all that had been prophesied in the Torah and by the prophets would be fulfilled. The young teacher endeavored to substantiate his claim by all manner of signs and miracles. And, in fact, this redeemer soon found a patient group willing to listen to his word. As long as Yeshua ben Josef wandered through the villages of Galilee with his band of simple farmers and fisherfolk, he was able to exert considerable influence on his listeners; but when he dared to appear in Jerusalem among the educated Jews, he was tried for blasphemy and executed.[70]

In itself, this pathetic story, like many another of its kind, might well have vanished in the desert of oblivion, and in fact his contemporaries took virtually no notice of the life and death of the divinely inspired carpenter from Galilee. But events developed otherwise. The small group of faithful, who had dispersed after his execution, began to gather again, and soon their influence began to spread by way of mysterious reports of the miraculous resurrection of the messenger of God. People like the fisherman Shimeon ben Jonah (Peter) testified that they had been present at the physical resurrection of the Messiah, and declared that he would come again to redeem the children of Israel.[71] By means of such reports and even more through miracles which they performed, the Apostles won the confidence and faith of a rising number of farmers and fishermen.

The higher classes of Jews also began to pay more attention to the new sect. The government authorities wanted to hear no more about the executed Yeshua's supposed mission, and they imposed heavy punishments on the faithful, which of course achieved the exact opposite of what they intended. One of the zealous persecutors of the Christians was a certain Saul of Tarsus, an educated man with a misguided faith in spirits and demons. One day Saul, later called Paul, had a vision which resulted in what was in effect a religious conversion. At one stroke, the fanatic enemy of the Galilean Messianic movement became its fanatic follower. With the entrance of Saul into the Jewish-Christian sect, a new element was introduced.

Saul threw himself into the movement with unparalleled zeal. The passion of his fanaticism flung germinal sparks into thousands of dry, world-weary, highly flammable souls. He turned to the cause of the prophet of Galilee, whom he knew only from hearsay, and was able to win adherents and recognition for the new sect in nearly all the countries of the Mediterranean. His missionary trips extended far beyond his native land. He traveled across Asia Minor, Macedonia, Greece and Italy, to make known first throughout the synagogues of the Jews only the arrival of the Messiah, the Christ. He, to whom his idol had appeared only in dreams, was a most devoted apostle of his Son of God. "I live," he said, "but it is not I; the Messiah lives in me." [72]

The Greeks were so intrigued by Paul's oratory that they mistook him for the god Mercury and insisted on offering up an ox in his honor.[73] Paul himself believed fanatically in the new Messiah and said that His followers were higher than the angels. (A peculiar statement in view of Paul's opinion of angels: he decreed that women be veiled so they would not be misled by angels.[74])

Paul's historical significance lies in his immense capacity for organization, to which the Christians were indebted for the rapid setting up of their church. He gained further recognition by his liberation of the Christian sect from Judaism. Originally adherence to Judaism was a prerequisite for acceptance of Christianity.

While Simon (called Peter) was still obliged to justify his friendship with Gentiles and swore that he did not break the dietary laws of the Torah, Paul dared to bring before the elders a proposal to do away with circumcision prior to Christian baptism.[75] The Jewish Christians held that faith in Yeshua as the Christus or Messiah was demanded by the Bible. Did not the Torah, as well as the prophets, foretell His coming? And Yeshua himself had said, "I come not to break the Torah but to fulfill it." And: "I am sent only to the lost sheep of Israel, and you should not cast my pearls before swine." By swine he plainly meant the non-Jewish population of Canaan. On these grounds the early Christians declared, "If you do not let yourself be circumcised according to the prescription of Moses, you will not be saved." [76] But by the time Paul made his proposal, there were already many Gentiles in the new sect, and his suggestion carried the day. With the omission of circumcision as a baptismal requirement, the break between Christianity and Judaism was complete. It was no longer possible for faithful Jews to heed doctrines that went against their cardinal laws. Thereafter, the two faiths went in diametrically opposite directions.

In time Judaism and Christianity became so hostile that in struggling against its progenitor, Christianity brought heavy accusations, to the effect that it owed its very existence to non-Jews, and that the Jews had been the only ones to oppose it! The truth is, however, that Paul, the actual founder of Christianity, believed in the superiority of the Jewish race, and admitted turning to the pagans only when he found his own people unwilling to accept the divinity of the Executed.[77] Christianity is a Jewish movement, Jewish in its ideas, Jewish in its teachings, Jewish in its sentiment, originating on Jewish soil. But by the time Constantine, the pagan protector of Christianity, named the Jews "murderers of the Savior," the keynote had been sounded for the subsequent tragedy of Jew-baiting.[78]

The simple character of the faith of the early Christians is unquestionable. Yeshua ben Josef appeared to them the sole born Son of Jehovah; yet they traced his lineage back to King David. They spoke much of wonders and miracles and promised themselves that the kingdom of heaven would come with Him, and that He would, in His own words, sit on the right hand of His Father in heaven and judge the twelve tribes of Israel. Paul was convinced of this: "Everything is created through Jesus, all things in heaven and on earth, all that is visible and invisible." Peter, who told Jesus, "Lord, you know all things," was also convinced of it. And lastly, Jesus, the man of Nazareth, was profoundly convinced of it, for he said of himself, "I and God are one." [79]

In the early days of Paul's influence, the Christians presented themselves as an orthodox Jewish sect who believed the word of the Apostles that Jesus was the real Messiah. In this sense they thought of themselves as true Israelites and observed the commandments of the Torah the same as their more skeptical brethren who were opposed to the Apostles.[80] The Jews, in turn, frequently discussed the status of their Christian brethren.[81]

The paths followed by Christianity after its severance from Judaism were very peculiar. Before its teachings had penetrated Western Europe, it had gained many adherents in Egypt and Asia Minor. The Mithra cult in Persia, the Isis cult in Egypt, indeed most of the Asiatic religions, had woven into their theology the myth of a virgin-born son of God.

In order to lend their own positions the glamour of mystery, many rulers took care to foster this belief in divine birth. Nothing was easier than to identify the legend-wreathed Jesus of Nazareth with the mythological son of God in a given cult. The propaganda of the Apostles fell on exceedingly fertile ground. Only at the walls of China, behind which the unfanciful mysticism of Lao-tse and the practical wisdom of Confucius reigned, and in India where the enlightened Buddha had already enjoyed half a millennium of divine adoration as a virgin-born son of God, where the Brahmans governed for centuries untold, was the propaganda of the Christian Apostles checked.

Side by side with the religious spirit, the Greek philosophy gained new authority from Neoplatonic Christian teachings in Egypt and the Levant. The need to reconcile faith with philosophy led to the formation of a whole series of world-views known under the general title of "Gnosis."

THE GNOSTICS

The origin of Gnosticism is to be found in the Jewish religious order of the Ophites (Brethren of the Serpent), who sought to combine non-Jewish elements of thought with the teachings of the Torah. In their opposition to temple services and the cult of sacrifice, the Ophites show affinity with the later Therapeutae and Essenes. The early Cabbala seems also to have sprung from them. Christian Gnosticism soon turned away from Judaism and developed, as in the case of Manichaeism, in diametric opposition to it. The Gnostics founded their teachings on early Jewish myths.[82] The names of the sects, of which Epiphanius numbers nearly fifty, suggest some of the sources of their thought. One was called the Sethian (from Seth) ; others, the Noahitic (from Noah), the Adamitic (from Adam), the Cainitic (from Cain), and so on. One was even called the Borborian (dung) sect because of the debauched life which its members led.

It would take us too far astray to elaborate on the varying world-views of the many Gnostic philosophers. For curiosity's sake, we shall mention only a few ideas of the Manichaeans. The central problems in their philosophy was the question of good and evil. They promised redemption from evil through the king of the Christ-Logos. The Jewish God plays a very unfavorable role in their mythology, and Persian and Indian ideas break through at every point. The whole system is a fanciful structure combining an aeon theory, an astrology, a theory of ecstasy, all based on theories of numbers.

The mythical founder of Gnosticism was Dositheus, teacher of the magician Simon Magnus, who was later elevated to godhood. He is said to have had twenty-nine and a half followers—the half being a woman!

The saner Christians immediately saw the danger that threatened their faith from these fanciful philosophers, and forcibly excluded them as heretics. Irenaeus, one of the leading apologists of Christianity against Judaism, branded the Gnostic prophets as fakirs who misled their followers by ghost stories and tricks based on their theories of numbers.[83] Irenaeus headed that church movement which, weary of disputations, endeavored to establish an incontrovertible dogmatism. Already the Christian Gospels had raised many obscure and vexing questions. According to Saint Chrysostom (347-407 A.D.), it was forbidden to question how a woman could have children and remain a virgin.[84] The problem of the virginity of the Holy Mother was especially perplexing to early Christianity.[85] Jesus is of divine origin, according to Anastasius, because "no one can claim human parentage when his body is derived, not from a man, but only from a woman." [86] The mass of contentious writings on this point are now virtually unreadable.

It is difficult to fathom the mentality of the metaphysicians and theologians of the early Christian era. One leading Christian thinker knows definitely that the Antichrist will be enthroned in the temple and rule Jerusalem for three years and six months; whereupon the Lord will come down from heaven and hold judgment. He will throw the Antichrist into hell and prepare the kingdom of redemption for the faithful.[87] Why the Lord must wait three years and six months before going into action against the sinful Devil remains unexplained. But perhaps it was easy to satisfy the demands for logic of an age which admired so highly the *"Credo quia absurdum"* of Tertullian. And besides, there was a weighty, practical reason for accepting the teachings of the Church: "The Lord will cleanse all heresies, even the church is cleansed by the holy spirit." [88]

Anyone curious about the limits to which belief could be pushed in those days should read the autobiography of Saint Hieronymus; he will learn amazing things! It seems, for instance, that the Devil once tempted Saint Phacon in the form of an Ethiopian girl, and the hard-beset saint was able to get rid of her only after boxing her ears. For two years thereafter he suffered an evil odor on his hand, in spite of the fact that immediately after the encounter he had repeated the Psalms in honor of Saint

Antonius for a whole day. Strange things were apt to happen in the early Christian churches. Saint Dorotheus never left his cell for fear of being led astray by the nuns. In addition, he was obliged to sit constantly by his window, to remind the virgins outside not to quarrel among themselves.

Largely under the influence of Philo, the apologists of the first few centuries A.D. spent their time trying to reconcile Greek and Roman metaphysics with Christian Gospel. In the fashion of phantasizing philosophers, they substituted the poor executed prophet of Galilee for the creative Logos, and transferred all the imagined powers of the Logos to him. Thus Athanasius said, "All who do not recognize God and do not honor His Logos, seem to me to be spiritually sick, for our all-redeeming Lord, Jesus Christ, through whom the Father cares for all, heals and sustains." [89] Further, all creation came into being through Jesus,[90] and "the Logos made it known that the evil among men can be forgiven only through His death." Since it was impossible for the immortal Logos to die, he had no other course than to take on a human body and through suffering human death, turn death away from the faithful.[91]

It was Clemens and Origen of Alexandria who, under the influence of Philo Judaeus, laid those foundations of Christian theology which for almost two thousand years were to be the bane of European philosophy. During that entire period, philosophy was to remain but a visitor—or a visiting servant, if you will—in the house of theology.

THE APOLOGISTS

These two tendencies of Christianity—its antipathy to ancient philosophy, on the one hand, and its effort to reinterpret ancient metaphysics in terms of its own teachings, on the other—continued until very recent times.

Those Christians who were philosophically learned during the first few centuries A.D. agreed to accept Jesus as

46

the universal Creator (Logos), who had already revealed himself, like the seed before the plant, prior to his earthly existence. Thus Justin Martyr, a Christian wearing a philosopher's cloak, declared that Plato was familiar with the Jewish Bible, even though he frequently misinterpreted it. Justin Martyr's prophecies regarding the millennium and the punishment of the wicked are easily traceable to their Greek sources.

The introduction of Greek philosophy into their faith caused the sincere Christians considerable problems. It was rather difficult to make proper use of the strained identification of the Judaic God with the creative Logos of Greek philosophy. While some thought of the Logos as a God-created thing having a personality distinct from that of the Creator, others tried to prove the complete identity of Father and Son. Even Irenaeus taught, Philo-like, that the Son (Logos) is born of God in eternity, is eternal and of God, though below God in rank. The Alexandrian Arius carried this a bit further and declared that the Son was not born in eternity, but had been God's first creation, and is therefore a separate being from the Father. This view found a zealous opponent in Anastasius (ca. 325), who came out on the winning side by getting his interpretation accepted at the politically powerful Synod of Constantinople. At this synod, the complete unity of Yeshua of Nazareth, with the Stoic concept of God, was established as a Catholic dogma, and as such it is accepted in the Catholic realm to this very day.

The injection of political motives into theological and philosophical disputes, as in the quarrel between Arius and Anastasius, is typical of subsequent Catholic dialectics. It need surprise no one that the early sincere and honest motives of the Church soon yielded to political and private pressures, and that the more it gained in secular power and unquestioning adherents, the more it lost in sincerity and integrity.

Of the many heresies of those days few could withstand the pressure of Catholic dogmatism. The Gnostic sect of

47

Manichaeans, traces of which survived till the thirteenth century, proved to be the most stubborn. The founder of the sect was the Persian Mani (executed in 276 A.D.), to whom are ascribed many religio-philosophic writings. Starting with the teachings of Zoroaster, Mani expounds the existence of a god of light and of a god of darkness whom he identifies with Jehovah.[92] Both rule regions rich in aeons and spirits. Each region is inhabited by different orders of spirits. The rulers of darkness run in the following sequence: the rulers of the deepest dark, those of the turbid slime, those of destructive storms, those of consuming fire, and those of dirty smoke. In this last region the Jewish God, the Lord of Awfulness, reigns.[93] The unsorrowing Jesus *(Jesus impatibilis)* inhabits the sun and moon, but for the redemption of the human soul he came to earth in the form of a man. Whoever does not purify himself on earth must undergo a cleansing process in the other world, carried out by the rays of the sun.[94]

Regarding the creation of man, Mani offers this ingenious interpretation of Genesis: In order to interfere in the world-plan of the God of light, the Devil married Sin and gave birth to Adam, the first man. Next Eve was born of the Devil's cohabitation with a female spirit. When the God of light sent Jesus in the guise of an aeon to warn Adam of the evil wiles of Eve, she and the Devil got together to produce Cain. Cain then lay with his mother, who gave birth to Abel. He lay with his mother again and this time she gave birth to two daughters, Worldlywise and Greed. Cain took his daughter Greed to wife, and Abel wedded his sister Worldlywise. Then an angel came down and lay with Worldlywise and she gave birth to two daughters, Kaufarjad and Barfarjad. Now Abel suspected all along that his father, Cain, was the parent of the two girls, so he picked a quarrel with Cain in which he got himself slain. In spite of all the warnings of the God of light, Eve seduced Adam and promptly gave birth to Seth. Thereupon Adam took his son Seth, along with Worldlywise and her two

48

daughters, and fled the kingdom of darkness. All of them then became the progenitors of the human race![95]

In their customs and sacraments, the Manichaeans differed little from the other Gnostic sects. They had dietary rules, fasts, and laws of abstinence on which they laid great stress. The Stoic division of mankind into the ignorant, the listeners, and the knowing is common among the Gnostics.[96] Mani introduced himself to King Sapur as a savior, which may have been the custom in prophetic circles in those days. The period was certainly crowded with redeemers, salvationists and the like. Along with other Gnostic leaders —such as Simon Magnus, Basilides (*ca.* 125), Montanus (*ca.* 155), Valentinus (*ca.* 150), Bardesanes (*ca.* 200)— Mani enjoyed godlike veneration.

AUGUSTINE

Early Christian philosophy found its most complete expression in the Numidian orator, Aurelius Augustinus (354-430), who became a bishop during his lifetime and was sainted by the Catholic Church after his death. Augustine assumed early a commanding position in Christian history, and is generally considered the most distinguished of the Church Fathers. His *Confessions* give us more than a little information about his private life, though the confessor is not always specific in describing his early pagan activities. The truth is that after a period of dissolute living Augustine was converted by the Ciceronian, Hortensius, to a belief to which he remained faithful to the end of his days. The Neoplatonism of Plotinus and the theology of Alexandria held a dominant place in his philosophy. An undertone of mysticism and the genuine pathos of his preaching won the former orator many adherents, especially among those who were more impressed by the emotional overtones than by the solid matter of a sermon.

Augustine's great work, *The City of God*, heralds the coming of the kingdom of Christ, when the undivided will of God will reign. Augustine divides history into six periods analogous to the six days of creation, the periods beginning with Adam, the Deluge, Abraham, David, the Babylonian exile, and the coming of Christ. After Christ's coming, no further progress may be expected in this world until the arrival of the kingdom of God, which is to be anticipated hourly.

Otherwise the *De Civitate Dei* is a compilation of essays intended to prove the superiority of the Christian religion to that of pagans, plus innumerable comments on the Gospels. A few of the chapter headings may suggest the character of this work so fundamental in Christian philosophy: "Concerning the difference of knowledge of the holy angels and that of the demons"; "Will the lean arise lean and the corpulent, corpulent on the day of judgment?"; "A consideration of the contention of the philosophers that earthly bodies cannot go to heaven because earthly things are drawn to earth by their own weight"; "Were Adam and Eve troubled by passion before they ate of the tree of knowledge?"; "Concerning the creation of the first few days which had morning and evening before the sun was as yet created"; "Concerning the kindness of good angels." [97]

What should be made clear is that Augustine taught nothing which might contradict the dogmas of the growing Catholic Church. He placed the authority of the Church Fathers far above reason, and held philosophy to be identical with Christianity.[98] He zealously defended the virginity of the Mother of God and dedicated an entire work to this beloved problem of Christian theology. He accepted Jesus, the Creator of the universe, as identical with God, and called him "the All-Knowing." But even in this he was not original.[99] It is a doctrine that has been endlessly repeated in the Church's articles of faith.[100]

How could the Church fail to recognize the merit of a bishop who stated: "He who is separated from the Catholic Church, no matter how praiseworthy his life, will not possess eternal life, but only the anger of God, even if only for this sin alone"? [101]

In himself Augustine combined pre-Christian philosophic-religious superstition with Christian myth in ideal proportions. He was convinced of the healing powers of relics as well as the resurrection of the dead performed by saints. He preached that man's real happiness is attainable only in the other world, a view shared later by Kant.[102] Like many Christians, Augustine was a pathological opponent of sexual intercourse; he disapproved of it even in wedlock, and urged all married people to turn to God for aid in their self-denial.[103] He defended with the greatest zeal the Catholic dogma that all mankind became sinful through the sexual sin of Adam and that this inherited stain can be removed only through the infinite mercy of God.[104] In case of need, however, *God can create men without resorting to sex,* as he had demonstrated in making Adam and Eve and in forming Jesus in the womb of a virgin. Augustine fearfully awaited the resurrection of the dead in the kingdom of God, though he did anticipate receiving a suitable reward for his devout Catholicism. He believed fanatically in the intercession of a third party before God, and once asked the people to pray for the soul of a baptized astrologer. He exercised his clerical right of confession with unexampled fanaticism, and shamelessly revealed the private lives of those who had entrusted their secrets to him in the process of exhorting his listeners not to repeat the same sins.[105] Thus he brought into the Church the method of denunciation which was to foster persecution and bloodshed for hundreds of years.

The only real good, he claimed, lay in obedience to the will of God as manifested through Catholicism. All evil is nothing more than the lack of this will, the absence of good. (*Cf.* Plotinus.) With the same zeal with which he fought doubt in the revelation of God to the Jewish people, he contended against the pagan belief that the world existed longer than was stated in the Jewish Torah. Completely convinced of the physical reality of hell, he maintained that it was as eternal as immortality.[106]

To complete the picture, we might add that Augustine

51

had been a member of the Manichaean sect for nine years, though after his break with it he fought the heretical group with all his might. Unstable of temperament, he was passionate in polemic as in life. Forever tortured by fear of the approaching judgment day, he exhibited occasional signs of skepticism. But no matter what he preached at the moment, his dogmatism never faltered. Incredibly arrogant, he was at the same time pathologically sensible; frank to the point of shamelessness; plagued by superstition and fear; yet an incomparably shrewd diplomat.

PLOTINUS AND THE NEOPLATONISTS

While the apologists and Church Fathers were working for the strengthening of the peculiar tenets of their faith, Greek philosophy, largely under Oriental influence, took a turn which led it ever deeper into mystic religiosity and phantasy. It lent itself rather easily to this transformation because of the vague and misty terms in which men like Pythagoras and Plato had cast their notions. Now superficial authors of popular essays continued to dilute its content.

Among the imaginative resurrectors of the Pythagorean spirit-world was a certain APOLLONIUS OF TYANA who lived in the days of Nero. He was sufficiently clever to acquire a reputation as a miracle-worker and descendant of the gods. A journey to the Orient had afforded him the opportunity to learn the prerequisites of his calling. Except for the addition of some Indian asceticism and the theory of the transmigration of souls, his teachings do not differ materially from those of other god-interpreters of his time.

Of the younger Neopythagoreans, NUMENIUS OF APAMEA (*ca.* 150 A.D.) laid special emphasis on the cult of demons and the art of soothsaying. He is the author of the famous dictum that Plato is only a Greek-speaking Moses. Leaning heavily on Philo Judaeus, Numenius developed further the concept of the trinity of the godhead, the cardinal principle of Catholic theology, which received a still more detailed formulation from the Egyptian Plotinus.

Egyptian Neoplatonism may be called the dying phase of Greek philosophy. Its founder was PLOTINUS OF ALEXANDRIA (204-270), a supposed pupil of the legendary Ammonius Saccas, of whom we know only that he favored a combination of the Platonic and Aristotelian philosophies.[107] So many of Plotinus' ideas are those of Numenius of Apamea that he was called the plagiarist of Numenius.[108]

The Plotinian philosophy is motivated by a desire to bring the uncharted religious ideas of the age under one unified system. However, instead of attaining understanding of these intricate dogmas, Plotinus let them lead him still deeper into confusion. We recognize here the kind of emotional obscurantism often found in religious metaphysics, whether it be the mysticism of a Heraclitus or Böhme. There are depths in human nature which are dangerous; they mislead their possessor into a self-abnegation based on the concept of a double self and a double soul. The almost inevitable insecurity to be found in thinking people has often enabled the makers of sects—and sometimes its exploiters—to bring thousands of the faithful into a state of personal subjection.

Plotinus, who like Apollonius of Tyana was often referred to as a charlatan, was in fact an astonishing man. "Very often," he said, "have I wakened out of my own body into myself. I reached into myself outside of all things, saw a wonderful beauty, certainly the finest yet conceived, which is attainable only through a unity with God, a unity which enables one to attain the highest form of life." [109] "Since evil reigns of necessity in this world, and the soul wants to escape evil, man must escape this world." [110] The other world is, of course, no other than Plato's world of Ideas, or Numbers which has remained a favorite place of escape even for modern philosophers. Plotinus claimed to have seen this world in moments of ecstasy, and he knew more about the lives of the gods than Plato's fallen Pamphylion, who arose twelve days after his death and related his experiences in the other world.[111]

What kind of creature Plotinus' ecstasy-inspired God may have been he leaves Philo to tell us. He is, in fact, different from all that is known, separate from all that exists. He is yet the Creator of all; He is creative yet undiminished; He is One. Out of God comes the Logos; out of the Logos, the world-soul and this is the philosophic trinity. The lower part of the world-soul emanates matter, which is evil. The better part of the soul emanates gods and star-spirits who exert a certain influence on man's fate. For this reason it is possible to read the course of human events in the stars. The lower part of the world-soul emanates demons who may take on bodies of air and fire, and whose habitat is the space between the stars and earth.[112] Plotinus sees such beautiful harmony in the world that he does not even consider it necessary to provide a good place for those who are evil. As with the Platonic soul, the better part of Plotinus' soul also had a pleasant pre-existence. After death, it returns to the "One," but first it must wander through various bodies, according to the measure of its virtue while on earth, before it is worthy to be admitted to the world of thought.

Plotinus' metaphysical speculations were further elaborated by his disciples. Among them, we should not overlook IAMBLICHUS, the famous Syrian magician, who aimed at bringing all the ancient polytheisms under one head. With the aid of the Plotinian theory of emanations and the Pythagorean system of numbers, he managed to corral all the gods of the ancient world under one hierarchy. Outdoing his master, he placed supergod over Plotinus' god of gods.[113] It is hardly possible to offer an orderly picture of Iamblichus' herd of deities. The heavenly gods alone number 360, while the lower and physical gods follow in 42 rows of 72 each, and below these are ranged a long chain of demons, angels and semigods. Iamblichus, who was an ardent defender of image worship, soothsaying and magic, received from his faithful the descriptive appellation, "The Godly."

PROCLUS OF BYZANTIUM (410-485), a teacher in the academy at Athens, was another Neoplatonist who burdened his listeners with extravagant accounts of his revelations. He too claimed to have heard voices from the other world, and the sayings of the oracles held special significance for him. Not satisfied with Iamblichus' museum of gods, he organized his own celestial system which later served both the Mohammedan and Christian theologies as a working model.

According to Proclus, the world-soul consists of three parts, the divine, the demoniac and the human. The divine part encircles a hegemony of twelve free, inner world gods, who contain among themselves the star-gods as well as the gods of nature. To fit this concept to the myths of the people, he invented a threefold Zeus and a threefold Athena.

Following Iamblichus, Proclus stresses five kinds of virtue which eventually culminate in the unity of God. Proclus laid the final stamp on Neoplatonism, and his formulation became the accepted one in the centuries that followed.

During the brief reign of the anti-Christian Caesar, Julian II, Neoplatonism received a new spirit of life, but it could not long survive before the growing numbers of Christian proselytizers. Further, there were so many points of contact between Greek philosophy and Christian theology that the absorption of one by the other went on steadily and imperceptibly. Thus the Neoplatonist, Synesius, could be appointed Bishop of Ptolomais without having to give up any of his former beliefs. Unfortunately, Christian missionaries were not always so tolerant, and theoretical differences not always settled by mere discussion. The fate of the learned Alexandrian pagan, Hypatia, who was mobbed to death at the instigation of Archbishop Cyril, is a case in point.

Justinian the Great finally decided that further open discussion of Catholic dogma could only be superfluous and dangerous, so he laconically forebade philosophizing of any kind. In 529, the philosophic academy at Athens was closed by imperial edict, and the last of the school's teachers fled to Persia.

DIONYSIUS THE AREOPAGITE

The quick recognition which Iamblichus and Proclus gained with their heavenly hierarchies was likely to suggest to Christian philosophers the creation of a similar system. That is exactly what occurred, around the fifth century A.D., to an Oriental metaphysician known to the Middle Ages as Dionysius the Areopagite.

Following the established models, Dionysius places Jehovah the Father, Jesus the Son, and the Holy Ghost, the triunity which controls the fate of man, at the head of Old and New Testament angels, cherubim and good angels. Three heaveny hierarchies come under the all-ruling God. The Seraphim, Cherubim and Thrones, who are immediately under God's care, take first place.[114] Next come the Dominions, Principalities and Powers. In the third place are the Virtues, Archangels, and ordinary Angels. This class arrangement, Dionysius declared, was set up by God and was intended for all eternity. In this kingdom, arranged with Byzantine perfection, each angel had his allotted task. Dionysius considered, for instance, that the angels were the authors of the Jewish Torah.[115] In the hierarchy of the Catholic Church, to which he dedicated a special work, he recognized a reflection of the heavenly hierarchy.

Like Plotinus, he saw in the arrangement of the world the good and wise predestination of God. Even the mighty devils, who are permitted to live by an all-wise Deity, are not really evil—they merely lack the good; they are fallen angels. The goal of the Dionysian hierarchy is the same as that of the Neoplatonic one, the unification of the individual soul with God. This may be attained in three ways: by the straight, the spiral or the central methods. Like Plato and the Neoplatonists, Dionysius prefers the mystic theology of negative description to a philosophy of positive speculation.[116]

Dionysius explains by more than sixty negative qualifications what God is *not,* and after he has counted up all that He is not, he warns the faithful against bringing their wisdom to the ears of the unfaithful. "Be careful," he wrote in his *Mystic Theology,* "that the uninitiated should not hear you; I mean those who are caught in the meshes of reality and fool themselves into believing that there is nothing more real than reality, those who believe they can conceive truth with their senses and have built their homes in darkness."

His style is characterized by the hyperbole and inflation of most mystics. At one point he prays to the "Super-being, super-divine, super-good trinity, protector of Christian wisdom, lead us to the upper, unknown, super-brilliant, all-highest acme of mystic expression, where the simple, absolutely unchangeable mystery of theology reveals itself in the pleasant, mystic silence of the super-light darkness which shines brightest in the darkest corner and fills the eyeless spirit with the invisible and untouchable dazzling of the super-beautiful." This is a persuasive argument for at least one of the philosopher's points: God must have indeed made darkness his dwelling place!

JOHN SCOTUS ERIGENA

The Irish priest, John Scotus Erigena (810-883), was the last herald of Neoplatonism. On the orders of Karl of Kahlens, he translated the works of Dionysius the Areopagite. The influence of the Areopagite on Erigena was so strong that Dionysian ideas invariably serve as starting points for his essays, and in his chief work, *The Divisions of Nature,* the master is cited on virtually every page. Erigena also leans heavily on the Greek Church Fathers, and in accepting their complete authority shows himself a forerunner of the Scholastics. For him, Plato was the great philosopher *(philosophantium de mundo maximus)*. But philosophy's highest task is to discover the real meaning of the Holy Scriptures, with which all inquiry should begin. For Erigena, the Gospels were the unalterable teachings of revelation.[117] It is not surprising, then, to read his dictum: "True philosophy is true religion." It goes without saying that by true religion he means the Catholic religion.[118] Although German philosophers have also asserted that religion and philosophy are one, they generally have had their eyes on the Protestant pulpit.

Like Plato, Erigena divided the world into three classes, which result in a fourth: (1) God, the uncreated Creator; (2) the Ideas or decrees of God, created and creating; (3) created and uncreating nature; and (4) God as the goal of all creation, uncreated and uncreating. Erigena pays his own tribute to the angels. He distinguished between nine choirs of them, divided into classes after the manner of Dionysius.[119] In contrast to Neoplatonic angels, however, those of Erigena lack the faculty of perception, though they have many visible beings among their company. Their degree of knowledge depends on their category. Ordinary, everyday angels, for instance, still have much to learn. Probably for reasons of morality, Erigena suggests that multiplication among angels takes place, not by means of sexual congress, but by fission.[120]

In spite of his good Catholic faith, Erigena never managed to gain the support of the official Catholic clergy. His very knowledge of Greek, which was despised in certain high ecclesiastical circles, made him suspect. Further, he incurred the Pope's disfavor by having his translation of Dionysius printed without proper Roman censorship. Finally, his contention with Gottschalk—a monk of the monastery at Fulda, who sponsored ultra-Augustinian doctrines regarding the predestined happiness of God's chosen, and the merciless damnation of the wicked—earned him the Church's lasting hostility, which ended in his excommunication and the burning of his works.[121]

ROSCELLINUS

The endless Platonizing of philosophers and theologians had long since been run into the ground in a tangle of contradictions. These conflicting assertions about the reality of the universals, the substantive, the super-real, and so on, had to end somewhere, even in this sterile period. Yet Erigena opened the way for still further disputation, and soon a grim battle was on between the "Realists" and the "Nominalists." The former asserted that the cloudy ideas of a super-reality were "real," whereas the latter insisted that such ideas were only concepts or "names."

The quarrel was more or less terminated by Canon Roscellinus (1080-*ca.* 1120), who applied the Nominalist theories to the divine trinity, thus disturbing the concept of a trinal divinity (*una substantia tre persona*) by boldly making it a combination of three polytheistic gods. Naturally, this Nominalistic interpretation raised a storm of protest. Roscellinus was forced to recant his thesis, and for a long time no one dared utter his doubts about the reality of the universal substances.

ANSELM OF CANTERBURY

We have had many occasions to observe how both the spirit of religion and that of philosophy have led the mind of man into empty speculations. With the combining of the two at the end of ancient times, complete stagnation in scientific inquiry set in. Cut off from Oriental stimulus by the victorious Mohammedans, bound by the chains of Catholic dogma, more misled than inspired by exhausted Greek philosophy, the culture of Europe went into almost total decline.

Savage tribes invaded the Roman countries and with nomadic shrewdness soon saw the possibilities for power latent in the Catholic Church. The cross offered the pretext of conversion as an ideal excuse for attacking one's neighbors. Soon all Europe echoed to the clang of the bloody swords of conversion-preaching barbarian princes. Thousands upon thousands poured out their blood for and against the cross which the robber barons wore on their shields. It seemed for a time that there might be no end to the slaughter. At last, however, the better sword prevailed, and the blood-stained cross was imposed upon the whole of Europe. The West had been "converted" to Christianity.

Thereupon independent investigation and thought came to an end. Philosophers were obliged to bow down before the cross. Ignorant mouths mumbled the prayers of Rome over the devastated earth. "Woe to our days," exclaimed Gregory of Tours. "All knowledge has declined." A single-minded hatred of knowledge threatened to destroy anyone who dared to undertake independent investigation. Rude barbarian lips repeated the words of Church Fathers who enjoyed divine adoration, and clung to such maxims as "Believe, that you may know!" [122] And the famous theologian, Anselm, who called for the death of Roscellinus, insisted, "I do not try to understand, because I believe; the more I believe, the more do I understand." For this affirmation of conformity he was in due time awarded the archbishopric of Canterbury.

Another teacher of that god-plentiful but reason-scarce time, the proselytizing preacher, Peter Damiani (1007-1072), insisted with unshakable certainty that logic cannot be applied to God because He can make that which has already happened as if it had not come to pass. This wonderful preacher did his best to spread the idea that philosophy is but the slave of theology.[123]

Among the zealots who disseminated the philosophy of the Church Fathers, Anselm of Canterbury (1033-1109) achieved a leading position. His major work is dedicated, in Augustinian fashion, to God Himself, whose wonderful attributes of kindness, justice, wisdom, omnipotence, and so on, Anselm managed to deduce. Catholic clericalism proved

60

not unappreciative of his devotions, and in due course advanced the worthy bishop to the ranks of the sainted.

Anselm's articles of faith are, by his own confession, merely repetitions of the dogmas of the Church Fathers.[124] "No Catholic Christian may doubt anything which the Catholic Church believes in and teaches," he proclaims. "If he can gain insight into the faith, he ought to thank God; if he cannot, he must not contradict, but bend his will and pray on." [125] Yet this man, who placed foolish superstition above all positive knowledge, dogma above understanding, and revelation above criticism, set himself up as the champion of speculative philosophy, as an investigator and lover of truth! [126] More astonishing still, traditional histories of philosophy have accepted him at his own evaluation.

In his well-known compilation of theistic epithets, Anselm allows himself this play of ideas: God is the greatest of all living things. But if God existed only in our imaginations, there would still be a greater being, a God in mind and in things *(in intellectu et in re)* ; therefore God exists.[127] His clever play on words has survived in the history of philosophy under the imposing title, "the ontological proof of the existence of God."

Anselm handled philosophical problems with professional ease. For instance: God, Jesus and the Spirit are one. All things that God has created existed first in His mind as ideas. God loves Himself, therefore angels and men were created to honor Him, though only the angels know this. The sole problem which seemed to trouble our philosopher was the question of original sin as it applied to angels, since they multiplied by fission.[128] In his *Cur Deus Homo* Anselm demonstrates that it was by absolute logical necessity that "God became a man and gave new life to the world through His death, although He could have done it through another person, such as a man, an angel, or even by his mere will." [129] In this same work he deduces that Mary the Mother of Christ must have been a virgin because Eve, the mother of the first sin, had been one.

61

Archbishop Anselm of Canterbury is generally considered the founder of medieval Scholasticism.

PIERRE ABELARD

The most intriguing representative of Platonic Catholicism was the French cleric, Pierre Abelard (1079-1142), more widely known for his unfortunate love affair with Héloïse. In his youth he had hearkened to both Roscellinus, the father of Nominalism, and William of Champeaux, the hard-headed protagonist of Realism. Choosing a compromise position, he preached neither the reality of universals nor the reality of single objects. Rather, he ascribed to universals a sort of prehistoric existence, declaring that before the creation they existed in the mind of God, whereas after the creation they subsisted in individual things. Such speculations regarding sacred dogma proved too daring for the Roman Church, however, and the poor preacher was persecuted relentlessly.

The Church disapproved of Abelard's logical explanation of revelation, above all because it threatened the supernatural authority of Church dogma. But Abelard exhibited a regrettable tendency to place common sense above the authority of the Fathers, and in his *Sic et Non* even tried to expose their contradictions on some of the most vital points of Catholic dogma.

Like many of his successors, however, Abelard failed to make a convincing plea for the investigation of true knowledge, for he went astray in his own fashion. It was his unstable, romantic character, his strong drive for honor and love, and, not least, his jealous rivalry with other preachers, rather than any genuinely revolutionary cry for common sense, which led to his persecution. After all, he was not veering from Catholic ground even in the act of trying to explain his position logically. He did not struggle against dogma for the sake of understanding; rather did he struggle with reason for the sake of dogma. Such remarks as that the trinal unity of God was known even to Plato, and that the Sybils emanated from the divine assumption of flesh, are as characteristic of Abelard as of his contemporaries. He believed that the trinity of God and the virginity of the Holy Mother were susceptible to logical proof, and drew up twenty-three tricky arguments to overwhelm those who doubted these dogmas.

His moral philosophy, marked by a tendency to subjective piety, rather than blind Catholic discipline, makes a quite sympathetic impression. Here again we find a Platonic influence, while his logic and dialectic are derived directly from Aristotle.

Up to the second half of the twelfth century, the Catholic metaphysicians had drawn their world-wisdom from the writings of Platonists and Neoplatonists, so that when the little-known ideas of Aristotle put in a reappearance, the Roman apologists made it their business to give their locked-up world system a thorough overhauling. Their approach to the Aristotelian renaissance was, of course, determined a priori by the limits of their religious organization.

It was the Jews and Arabs who, at this time, brought the almost forgotten writings of Aristotle to the startled attention of the scholars of Rome. With the discovery of their ignorance in the face of this revival of the Greek spirit, the clerical world set to work on the rediscovered physical, metaphysical and ethical theories, and they continued their efforts until Aristotle had been swallowed and digested in his entirety. Their most difficult task was reconciling the strange, and in many ways unfriendly, Aristotelianism with the principles of Platonic Catholicism. Some believed that the strongest Catholic argument, that of excommunication, should be applied against the Aristotelians, but a few illustrious minds succeeded in attaching both heads to one body. The great masters of this metaphysical fusion were Albertus Magnus and Thomas Aquinas.

With great ingenuity these two metaphysicians discovered a large number of Catholic principles in the writings of

Aristotle, and soon the latter had dispossessed Plato as the philosophic ancestor of the Church. Thus the erstwhile tutor of world-conquering Alexander became "the" philosopher of "the only true Church" and the mainstay of Scholasticism. In him, said Albertus Magnus, nature had reached its highest peak of perfection, while Roger Bacon compared him to the Apostle Paul.

But while Aristotle is bringing new knowledge to Christian Rome, we must go back and examine earlier developments in Arabian and Jewish philosophy, which became the carriers of the new enlightenment.

MOHAMMED IBN-ABDALLAH

It was in the year 570 of the common era that the founder of a new religion, Mohammed, son of the poor merchant Abdallah and his sickly wife Amina, saw the light of day in the little business town of Mecca. The boy's parents died early, and he came under the care of relatives who, though he had suffered from epileptic attacks since his fourth year, used him for the worst kind of menial labor. This arduous life affected the boy's constitution, and he began to have hallucinations which, though disappearing at the onset of adolescence, recurred later in severe form.

At the age of twenty-five the boy, now a camel driver, came into the employ of the widow-merchant Khadija, who offered her fifteen-year-younger employee both heart and hand. It is uncertain what motives led the young camel driver to accept the elderly widow, who is reputed to have been uncommonly ugly, but the record states that, barely a month after her death, Mohammed married another, equally wealthy widow. The inherited business enterprises of his first wife freed Mohammed from all further material worries and permitted him to enter a state of blessed idleness.

Through his contact with Jewish and Christian merchant-travelers, Mohammed acquired information on Jewish-Christian mythology. How superficial his knowledge must have been is suggested by the earnestness with which scholars have applied themselves to the question whether he could even write. The angel lore so widespread in his time seems to have had a special appeal for him, and it is hardly surprising that when the seizures of his youth began to recur, Mohammed connected them with his mythological dream world.

An indescribable sadness and a deep anxiety that he might be possessed of evil spirits overtook the ill youth. He fell prey to his frightening disease in the hot, glaring fields outside Mecca. One seizure followed another. Chills turned to fever, which was followed by convulsive cramps that brought about utter exhaustion. After such attacks, he was found with foam-covered lips, unable to move, and troubled by the vague remembrance of strange noises and voices. Weeping and wailing, Mohammed plagued his friends with stories about the spirits that had visited him. They tried to calm him by arguing the harmlessness of the visions, until his wife dropped certain hints about the possibility of a divine mission for her husband. Her remarks fell on fertile soil.

On the night of the twenty-third and twenty-fourth of the month Ramadan in the year 611, the angel Gabriel appeared to Mohammed, son of Abdallah, and announced the glad tidings: "There is no God but God, and Mohammed is his prophet." Mohammed's fate was sealed. He hurried to his relatives and, full of gladsome fear, proclaimed what had happened. Thereupon his wife and child bowed down before him and called out, "Praised be the prophet of God!" Among the first to believe in his calling were his friend, the shrewd Abu-Bakr, and his adopted son Ali.

The first revelation was followed by a second and third, and finally an endless chain of them. Progressing in his visions to the seventh heaven, he there met Abraham who he discovered bore a striking resemblance to himself. There he also spoke with God, who commanded that people should offer Him fifty prayers daily. However, after counseling with Moses, whom he met on his way back through the sixth heaven, and after considerable bargaining, Mohammed obtained a reduction of the daily prayers to five.[130]

The revelations followed one another so rapidly that even some of the faithful became worried. They learned of seven heavens and seven earths, of two black angels who judged departed souls, and of many other marvels.[131] Mohammed interpreted the Torah and the Gospels in terms of his own mission as the Messiah. To this end he made known the following prophecy: "Those to whom we have given the Torah and the Gospels should be converted to Mohammedanism. The faithful will be rewarded well, but the punishment of the unfaithful is the fire of hell." [132] The threat of hell is as ever-present with Mohammed, and also the province of paradise where the prophet assured his faithful of "food and drink and soft beds and lovely young women with beautiful eyes." The expectation of meeting seductive houris after death was not without appeal to Bedouins contemplating conversion to Mohammedanism.[133]

Mohammed represented himself as the last prophet and the true Messiah, of whom all preceding prophets were merely heralds.[134] Similarly, he forgave all sins committed before his coming, whereas sins committed against his prophecy were unforgivable. As for himself, he explained that in his youth two angels had opened his heart and removed the bitter drop of original sin.

Faith in Mohammed was for a few years limited to a small group of families. So far the cult had not been born. It was built later as a defense against the unfaithful, and consisted chiefly, besides the above-mentioned five daily prayers, in abstinence from swine flesh and the blood of animals, as well as in certain rules for fasting borrowed for the most part from Mosaic ritual. The main rite was adapted from the old heathen custom of praying at the Kaaba, a large hut in the large *Moschee* at Mecca, into which had been built a stone the Arabs believed Abraham had brought from heaven with the assistance of the angel Gabriel. As ruler of Mecca, Mohammed circled the hut seven times, according to the ritual law.

One of the many who had only contempt for Mohammed's efforts was his uncle, Aba Lahab, who dismissed him summarily as a fool. For this Mohammed paid him off with a picturesque curse: "May the hands of Aba Lahab rot, let them rot! His riches will not help him. He will burn in hell fire, the flames of which will never be extinguished; and together with him will be his wife. He will have to bring the wood himself, and a rope will hang about his neck." This thrilling prophecy makes up the 111th Sura of the holy Koran.

The real character of Mohammed became evident only after the death of Khadija. Troubles in Mecca obliged him to leave town in a hurry with all his belongings on the sixteenth of July, 622 (the beginning of the Mohammedan calendar). Settling in Yathrib, which his disciples call Al-Medina, he started his campaign against the unfaithful, taking advantage of standing feuds between Arab tribes. In true Bedouin fashion, he raided caravans and attacked villages, either massacring the inhabitants or carrying them off into captivity. According to Bedouin law, a fifth of all the loot went to Mohammed. Runaways were left in the desert with amputated hands and blinded eyes, and it was forbidden even to give them a drink as they perished under the sizzling desert sun. The stories of his brutal conduct are endless. "Drive all the unfaithful out of Arabia," he ordered, "and slaughter every Jew who comes into your hands." [135]

At this period of his mission, Mohammed appears to us little more than a barbaric Bedouin chieftain. A disorderly mob, of whom the old writers say that they clutched their rags about them to hide their nakedness, rallied beneath his banner to fight for the self-proclaimed prophet of God.

"My only pleasures on earth," said the prophet, "are women, fine odors and prayers." Concerning the prayers we know little; but the odor of his interest in women could not be concealed by all the spices of Arabia. At the age of fifty-five he married the nine-year-old daughter of his friend Abu-Bakr. From year to year his harem grew. When his wife-stable could no longer accommodate the influx of wives, he disposed of the excess among the faithful. "Women are your plows," he said. "You can order them as you will." No woman was safe from his demands. "The prophet needs more women than other men," the angel Gabriel had revealed to him. [136] Gabriel had made still another concession: "If a married woman offers herself to the prophet, the prophet may take her, but that is forbidden to other Moslems."[137]

This man compelled his adopted son to turn over his wife for his jaded pleasure. This annoyed even the Arabs, who were not unfamiliar with such by-play. "God wills it," Mohammed answered. "The angel Gabriel has revealed it to me."[138] He brought Rahina, the wife of a brutally murdered Jew, to his own bed on the day of her husband's execution. To another Jewess, Kafiyya, whose husband had been beaten to death, he offered the alternative of giving herself to him or going into slavery. At the age of sixty he was caught *flagrante delicto* with a slave girl in the bedroom of one of his wives. When the wife reprimanded him, he was cowed at first and swore never to touch the slave again; but on thinking it over, he happily remembered that Gabriel had revealed to him: "O Prophet, why would you deny yourself that which God has permitted you?" [139]

Such was the life and such the teachings of Mohammed son of Abdallah. The father-in-law of the prophet continued his march of conquest and spread the kingdom of the faithful to the shores of the Atlantic. Mohammed's teachings and prophecies, carefully gathered by his followers, became the pivot and starting point for new speculations in Arab philosophy.

AL-FARABI

East Arabian philosophy took a course similar to that of Catholic philosophy. After many unsuccessful efforts to combine the Koran with Greek philosophy, Arabian thought was finally throttled by orthodoxy. The various sects among the faithful fought among themselves with the same zeal as the Catholics in the West. The quarrel between Augustine and Pelagius over the kindness and justice of God has its exact counterpart in the struggle between Mutazilla and al-Ghazzali over predestination and the mercy of God.

The first noteworthy Arab philosopher to make his influence felt was al-Farabi (Abu Nasr Mohammed ibn-Mohammed ibn-Tarkan Uzlag of Farab in Turkestan, died 950). He continued the translation of Greek works into Arabic, which had been initiated by the physician al-Kindi. Al-Farabi became known as "the second master," the title of "first master" going to Aristotle. Al-Farabi championed the authenticity of certain pseudo-Aristotelian writings on theology which, in the nineteenth century, were proved to be selections from Plotinus.

The philosophy of the Arabs must relinquish every claim to genuine originality. On closer examination, their works turn out to be a superficial rehash of Neoplatonic and Aristotelian ideas, and are of interest only because they are interwoven with Mohammedan lore.

In the religious disputes which had started somewhat earlier, al-Farabi joined the side of al-Ghazzali, for he was convinced of predestination as it was taught in the Koran. "God knows before hand," he said, "that the man whose obedience he has decreed will be obedient. Further, God knows that once one or another has stepped into Paradise, He will not send him back to hell." [140] Al-Farabi establishes the authority for his science as follows: He received it from the Koran of the prophet, the prophet received it from the angel, and the angel had it from God. Al-Farabi, then, had good reason to suppose he would be rewarded with direct contact with God on the day of judgment.[141]

Since he enjoyed this close relationship with the Deity, it should not surprise us to find al-Farabi a Sufist of the Islamic herd. Al-Farabi nursed Greek philosophy alongside the Koran, as the Christians combined it with the Gospels.

In the realm of fancy, contradictory facts are easily brought into harmony, and agreements are easily rendered incompatible.

As a moral philosopher, al-Farabi, in his *Elements of Conduct,* offers those who wish to live the good life advice which shows his true leanings: "One offers up praise to the ruler by praising all that he undertakes, large or small, and by making an effort to find the good side of everything he may say." "One should belittle oneself before the ruler as if he could deprive one of all goods and wealth without effort."[142] What a conception of human self-respect!

AVICENNA

Ibn Sina (Avicenna, 980-1037), court physician to many small princes in Khurasan, was dependent in much of his thinking on the Aristotelian and Neoplatonic ideas of al-Farabi. The medical canon of this man, who claimed to have completed his secular education at the age of eighteen, carried unlimited authority in the West as well as the East until the coming of Paracelsus (1530).[143]

With al-Farabi, Avicenna taught the planting of the "first intelligence" in various spirits in the spheres and in man. The soul of man has two faces, one turned toward the body, the other toward the "prime intelligence." [144] The soul, of course, returns to the "prime intelligence" after death. Even at the time of Judah ha-Levi, Avicenna still passed as a leader of philosophy.[145]

Also flourishing at the time of Avicenna was the philosophic order of "Pure Brethren," who contrived commentaries on the more daring Suras of the Koran with the help of Pythagorean number theories and Talmudic allegories. They taught that the seven planets which rule the lives of men could also predict the future. They differentiated between good and bad planets and gave each a special function. Belief in life after death, paradise and hell, resurrection on the day of judgment, as well as the necessity of unlimited asceticism in this world, were some of the articles of faith of this religious order.

AL-GHAZZALI

The mystic, Abu-Hamid ibn-Mohammed al-Ghazzali of Tus in Khurasan (1058-1111), appeared toward the end of this period of East Arabian philosophy. Al-Ghazzali's visionary temperament led him to give up his scientific work to become a wandering preacher of Mohammedanism. Upon joining the Sufi sect, he returned home to spend the remainder of his life in prayer and religious observances.

In his ecstatic devotion to the Koran, he sought to defend its prophecies against all philosophic doubt. Under the influence of Greek philosophy, he wrote a book on *The Destruction of Philosophy*, in which he contended that philosophy contradicted the Koran on three points: resurrection, predestination and the day of judgment. In a later work, *The Revival of Religion*, he accepted philosophy as a preparation for theology.

Al-Ghazzali claimed that the laws of nature are not sufficient explanation of the world because the least event is immediately determined by God. A leaf does not fall from the tree without His express command. Should God will it, oil would not burn. Since God is not bound by natural law, the miracles related in the Koran are not contradictory to the laws of nature.

This type of philosophizing earned for al-Ghazzali the contemporary sobriquet, "the Proof of Islam."

In time, this philosopher was completely engulfed by the superstitions of Islam. He demanded from the Moslems strict observance of prayers, fast days, litanies, pilgrimages, etc.[146] "Do not delay to recite the prescribed Suras for Friday, it is very important." "Allah should be mentioned in every action; every deed should be brought into close relation with him." "Do not forget to cleanse your teeth; that cleanses the mouth and arouses the pleasure of

71

God and the anger of the devil." [147] Even in fulfilling natural needs, Allah must be praised: "When you enter the place of privacy put your left foot forward and, in going out, put your right foot forward." "Upon leaving say, 'Allah Akbar, praised be Allah who let that which is harmful pass from me and let that which is useful remain.' " [148] Even in the bridal bed the name of Allah should be invoked: "When you cohabit with your wife, in the moment of embrace exclaim, 'Allah Akbar, God is great!' " [149]

In his *Gems of Knowledge* one may read what al-Ghazzali knew about life after death. The soul of the departed is the size of a bee. If it be sinless, it is rolled up in silk by two well-dressed angels and wafted up to heaven. An evil soul, on the other hand, is packed in coarse sackcloth by two repulsive angels and tossed into hell.

The theology and philosophy of the Koran straitjacketed the cultural life of the Near East for centuries, choking every effort at reform at its very center. Only in recent years have steps been taken toward the emancipation of Asia from its retarding superstitions.

AVERROES

The Mohammedan countries of the West produced little original thought beyond the dry academicism of scholars, the natural consequence of an era of theological domination.

Avempace, ibn-Tufail and Averroës stand out from the Platonizing Aristotelians of the Western Arabs. The first of these (Abu-Bakr Mohammed ibn-Bajjah, 1100-1138), a contemporary of Abelard, wrote a *Guide to the Lonely*, in which, following al-Ghazzali's example, he offers directions for attaining the Platonic unity with God, plus a series of commentaries on Aristotle. The second, ibn-Tufail (Abu-Bakr ibn-Tufail Alkasi, 1100-1185), is known for a romance about the autodidactic philosopher which aims to show the relation between philosophy and religious conventions.

Ibn-Tufail, however, paved the way for the popularity

and influence of Averroës (Abu-al-Walid Mohammed ibn-Ahmad ibn-Rushd, 1126-1198). He urged Averroës to write commentaries on Aristotle, since for all Arabian philosophers Aristotelianism was *sapiens divina* (divine wisdom), representing the summit of human knowledge, as the Koran represented the ultimate in law and morality.

Averroës, described as "the crown of Arab wisdom," accused al-Farabi, al-Ghazzali and especially Avicenna, of misrepresenting Aristotelianism. Yet Averroës himself considered the sciences merely arts, that is, bodies of knowledge separate and complete, which need only be "handed down." [150] He remained a total stranger to real Greek culture and knew Aristotle only through faulty Syrian and Arabic translations.

Like Avicenna, whom he criticized so vigorously, he clung to the belief that the heavenly spheres are controlled by "intelligence." The prime intelligence is God, whom the other angelic intelligences serve as slaves. Averroës concedes that each sphere soul possesses a mind and an eternal existence, though in contradiction to Avicenna, he denies it the organs of sense. He also denies it the power of feeding and reproducing.[151] The concept of matter rising up to God as the soul descends from the heavens to unite with it and form man, is one of Averroës' favored ideas.

Averroës looks to the Koran for proof of the existence of God.[152] His thinking never freed itself from either the Koran or the Aristotelianism of his day. As a well-known Arabist has said, "Arab philosophers are the beggars of Aristotle to whom they were introduced through Neoplatonic commentaries." [153]

SAADIA BEN JOSEPH

The philosophy of the Arabic Jews was likewise little more than religious exegesis. The same Aristotelianism and Neoplatonism served them in explaining the texts of the prophets and in rationalizing religious dogmas.

73

Not merely their principles of faith, but the smallest of their precepts, every utterance of the Toraic writings, every act and miracle of their holy ones, must be proved to be philosophic truth. The Gospels may deny what the Torah asserts, the Koran may condemn what the Gospels sanction, the prophets may contradict each other but philosophy proves them true.

Rabbi Saddia ben Joseph of Fayun (892-942) was the first of a series of Jewish philosophers to feel the influence of Arab orthodoxy. Among his writings, all of which treated Biblical subjects, his chief work, *Faiths and Philosophies*, gained a wide audience.

In the very introduction of *Teachings of the Faith* Saadia makes it clear that the book is dedicated to the philosophic justification of the Torah. His arguments are taken from both philosophy and the Torah: one assumption is proved by another. Saadia was convinced of the literal truth of every sentence in the Torah. He believes in corporeal resurrection, stating that the soul floats above and around the corpse until the time it rejoins it. He believes in bodily hell and paradise and in the judgment day, when the pious will rise up out of their graves upon the arrival of the Messiah. He believes in two kinds of angels: momentary ones, created for a single act, such as those created for the persuasion of a prophet; and eternal ones, who have constant contact with God. The body of an angel is made of such fine matter that it is invisible to the human eye, though the angel of death may appear as a green fire shot through with fearful eyes, the sight of which brings instant destruction.[154]

The sole task of philosophy is to prove this celestial world. Philosophy must substantiate what we know already from the teachings of the prophets. For instance, it is written that in the beginning God created heaven and earth. The philosophic proof of this is: Earth is infinite, therefore it must have been created by God out of nought; it is finite because it is in the center of the universe, encircled by the heavens.[155] Likewise, the proof of the immortality of the soul: The Torah teaches that God is just; but since adequate reward is not received on earth, life must be prolonged in a hereafter where, by means of heaven and hell, justice can be achieved. Immanuel Kant repeated this philosophic proof verbatim, as a postulate.[156]

BACHIA BEN JOSEPH

Rabbi Bachia ben Joseph ibn-Pakuola (*ca.* 1100), who in *Duties of the Heart* cloaks the Torah and Talmud in an ecstatic piety by which "every man sees without eyes and hears without ears," [157] was a successor of Saadia. His work is based entirely on Plotinus' supposition of a dual soul, one part of which is bound to matter, the other to God. Like al-Ghazzali, Bachia would make philosophy the handmaiden of religion. Knowledge to him meant knowledge of God, and this knowledge was contained in the Torah, written by God Himself, for the Jews and for the Jews only.[158]

SOLOMON IBN-GABIROL

History played Catholic philosophy a mean jest in Solomon ibn-Gabirol (1021-1058), a composer of Hebrew liturgical songs. His work, *The Source of Life,* published over the name of "Avicebron," played a leading role in Christian Scholasticism, and influenced philosophers unaware of its author's Jewish origin.[159] Ibn-Gabirol was the only Jewish philosopher of the Middle Ages who took his arguments from neither the Torah nor the Talmud. His thought was determined entirely by Neoplatonism, and he was upbraided by earlier Jewish historians for lack of faith in the Torah.

Ibn-Gabirol subscribed to Plotinus' theory of emanations, but wishing to keep God and the world separate, he created a host of intermediary beings through whom the will of God might express its creative power.[160] The mystic interpretation of the will of God is to be found in the early

Cabbalistic book, the *Zohar*, where the will, after revelation, creates pure celestial forms.[161] In Gabirol, also, "matter emanates out of the infinite in an incomprehensible manner," as incomprehensible, indeed as the "absolute quiescence" of Schopenhauer's "Will." Ibn-Gabirol's rather indefinite style invited many misinterpretations of his thought. Bruno considered him a pantheist.

Abuse of the word "God" is, however, only too common in philosophy. God has been, on occasion, "spirit," "will," "soul," "nature," "love," and so on.

In Catholic circles *The Source of Life* aroused lively controversy, but it met with little success among the Jews, perhaps because of its ambiguity.

JOSEPH IBN-SADDICK

Another representative of the numerous Platonizing Jews is Rabbi Joseph ibn-Saddick of Cordova (died 1149). After the fashion of the Arab philosophers, he demonstrated in his *Microcosm* the parallelism between man and the world.[162] His definition of matter as self-subsisting substance (for which he did not claim originality) is to be found, with the same descriptive term, *"generis causa sui,"* in Baruch Spinoza.[163] Spinoza also studied the Bible exegesis of another Jewish Neoplatonist, Abraham ibn-Ezra (1088-1163).

ABRAHAM IBN DAVID HA-LEVI

Rabbi Abraham ibn David ha-Levi earned his fame by introducing a new trend into Jewish religious philosophy. His approach was to attempt verifying the ideas of Aristotle by the teachings of Moses.

His main concern was with the familiar question: Are the actions of man predestined by God? As an orthodox Jew, he begins with the teachings of the Torah, which he considers proven by six hundred thousand proofs, and uses Mosaic postulates to confirm Aristotle's assumptions.

Although he believes the truth was revealed to Israel before all other nations, he does not refrain from calling Aristotle and his Arab commentators the true philosophers. Yet all knowledge serves only for the interpretation of the Torah, just as the highest goal of philosophy is the support of the Ten Commandments. Since Moses, Jewish tradition has been incontestable. The center of the spiritual world is the Torah, the center of the physical world is Palestine, the land from which God selects his prophets. Like ibn-Sina, ibn David assumes the planets to be living beings endowed with understanding who exist only to serve the glory of God.[164]

MOSES BEN MAIMON (Maimonides)

Moses ben Maimon of Cordova (1135-1204) exerted considerable influence on Christian philosophy. Driven from his home town in his youth, he fled to Morocco where for a very brief time he was converted to Mohammedanism. From there he fled to Egypt where, as physician to the Sultan Saladin, he devoted himself entirely to Jewish national and religious affairs.[165] His greatest desire was to bring the Jews closer to the Torah and the Talmud. To achieve this, and yet retain the approval of the many Jews educated in Islamic schools, he tried, as Philo had done a thousand years before, to explain the Torah and Talmud *ex ratione*.

The revelations of the Jewish prophets were as unalterable to him as was the philosophy of Aristotle, his personification of wisdom. When a citation from the Talmud did not appear compatible with Aristotelian philosophy, Rabbi Moses had recourse to philosophic allegory. Thus the four wings of angels mean the four principles of motion of the spheres; the four angels Jacob saw going up and down the ladder are the four elements; Abraham the patriarch becomes the Aristotelian idea of form, and his wife Sarah the concept of matter.[166]

Rabbi Moses' chief work was the systematic arrangement of Jewish traditional law.[167] His *Guide to the Perplexed* was intended to bring doubters back to the path of the Torah, while his work on logic served to explain philosophic terms.

Rabbi Moses' orthodoxy is illustrated by his branding as a renegade beyond salvation, anyone who claimed that so much as a single word of the Torah was written by Moses rather than at the express dictation of God. He applied the same judgment to those who denied the resurrection of the dead or doubted the coming of the Messiah and the day of judgment. "Whoever," he said, "does not believe in even one command of the Torah will not have the world to come." [168]

His logic is that of the Torah, his thought that of the Talmud. He read Aristotle in the spirit of the Torah and interpreted him in terms of religious symbols. Moses ben Maimon succeeded as few before or after him in uniting knowledge with faith, for his knowledge depended on his faith, and in his faith he found profound knowledge.[169]

JUDAH HA-LEVI

Judah ha-Levi ben Samuel of Castile (1085-1140) also tried, in his *Defense of the Abused Religion,* to turn philosophy to the service of the Mosaic faith. Claiming that true prophecy and knowledge were given only to the Jews as the descendants of Shem, he said that all other peoples (including Aristotle) lack knowledge and truth for they are the descendants of Japhet. Whatever philosophers and investigators seek regarding the laws of morality or the laws of nature, is to be found in its most perfect expression in the Torah.[170] All other philosophy exists only as a preparation for the wisdom of the Torah.

Post-Maimonidean philosophy among the Jews assumed

the form chiefly of commentaries. Only occasional figures, such as Rabbi Moses ben Nachman of Geronna (Nachmonides), Rabbi Levi ben Gershon of Bangol (Gersonides), and Rabbi Chasdai Crescas, achieved exceptional influence. At the end of the fifteenth century Spanish Catholicism drove the Jews out of Spain, and with this exile from their second homeland, the history of medieval Jewish philosophy comes to an abrupt end.

ALBERTUS MAGNUS

As we have noted, it was through Jewish and Arab translations that Aristotle was introduced into Western Catholicism. Aristotelian philosophy, which at first found little favor, came eventually to supplant the once popular Platonism. Pioneer in this movement was a German monk, Albertus (1193-1280), later bishop of Regensburg, whom a dazzled generation called *"doctor universalis"* and *"doctor magnus,"* and finally "Albertus Magnus."

It was Albertus who succeeded in proving two untruths by three contradictions. First he separated theology from philosophy, declaring that the former, being a matter of revelation, was far above human understanding.[171] But at the same time he asserted that since both come from the same source there can be no contradiction between them. Moreover, theology should be substantiated by reason; first, in order that it may be better understood; secondly, "that it may be more worthy of belief"; and thirdly, "that it may be better defended against unbelievers." [172] Yet certain revealed mysteries, such as the dogma of the trinal unity, transubstantiation, the immaculate conception, resurrection, and so on, must remain untouched by philosophy.

Aristotle was called by the Scholastics the precursor of Christ *in naturalis*, in distinction to John, whom they called the precursor of Christ *in gratuitis*. Albertus himself called Aristotle the most perfect of men, and was careful not to contradict him in the smallest particular. In psychology and logic, even in what he called "natural science," he did not go beyond commentary on his pagan master and the latter's Jewish and Arab annotators.

Whereas Aristotle, however, gave eternal life to only a portion of the soul, Albertus was obliged, in support of the Catholic dogma of salvation, to attribute immortality to the whole soul. In treating this subject, he makes the original statement that the soul of the departed is like an angel.[173] By order of Pope Alexander IV, Albertus composed thirty-six arguments in proof of immortality.

In his moral philosophy, Albertus absorbed the four virtues of the Greeks into the three of the Church, faith, love and hope; hope, he said, can be achieved only through the intercession of the Holy Ghost. In the empty argument over universals, he took the compromise position of allowing them to exist in, before and after real things. Certain secular writings of his, such as an alphabetic register of the healing properties of gems, later caused numerous books on magic and related subjects to be ascribed to Albertus.

THOMAS AQUINAS

The Italian, Thomas of Aquino (1225-1274), *"princeps scholasticorum"* and *"doctor ecclesias et angelicus,"* a pupil of Albertus Magnus and patron saint of all Catholic schools since 1880, completed a carefully planned revision of Albertian philosophy.

Thomas followed his master in all things except natural science, where he was less adept than Albertus. He too was convinced that philosophy must not contradict revelation,[174] and that both led to the same goal.[175] The most convincing of his arguments for the truth of revelation relate to miracles and prophecies. The norm of his philosophy is, of course, the Catholic faith. True knowledge is philosophy, but man can achieve it only in the world to come *(visio beatica)*. Since it is unattainable in this world, man must accept the supernatural teachings of revelation.[176] In the more delicate questions of purgatorial cleansing, original sin, resurrection and creation, Thomas leans heavily on Albertus Magnus, as Albertus leaned on Rabbi Moses ben Maimon.[177]

As a disciple of Aristotle, Thomas conceives the ideal state as an inherited monarchy which caters to the Catholic well-being of its subjects. In this sense the ruler of the state is the representative of God on earth. This larger responsibility gives kings greater claim to honor and indulgence, and greater reward in the world to come. Thomas urgently warns the people against revolution and the sinful murder of tyrants. He advises them to rely rather on the mercy of God, who in time of real need will interfere more swiftly, the more virtuously and faithfully they have conducted themselves.[178]

In true apostolic fashion, Thomas assigns to women a subordinate role in life. He calls them unsuccessful men *(vir occasionatus)*, in spite of the fact that God made Adam and Eve personally, without intermediary, according to pre-existent idea.[179]

This is another of the areas in which philosophy has done not a little to retard social advancement. Schopenhauer considered women unfit to hold political office, while Fichte taught that a woman's duty is to obey, first her father and then her husband. Even in our time the chains of religious and philosophic prejudice against women have not been entirely abandoned.

The philosophies of Albertus and Aquinas enjoyed wide influence in their time and continue to do so to this very day. On the eighteenth of November, 1907, Pope Pius X reminded teachers "to keep to the foundation laid down by Saint Thomas from which one cannot deviate even in the slightest matter without much harm, especially in matters of metaphysics." [180]

JOHN DUNS SCOTUS

The intellectual tendencies of Dominican philosophy called forth objections from many Catholic leaders. The most zealous protests came from the Franciscan order, which laid great stress on the ascetic principles of the Church. Their most prominent spokesman was the Irishman, John Duns Scotus (1265-1308), who in 1304 received the title, *"doctor subtilis,"* thanks to his successful defense of the "virginal conception" of the Holy Mother. Duns Scotus, a fanatical observer of all Church decrees, was ardent in his attack upon the overvaluation of natural reason. Leaning heavily on the Jewish philosopher, ibn-Gabirol (Avicebron), he argued the superiority of the will over the intellect.[181] Man's highest duty is the subjection of his will to "the true church," not the independent search for truth. Theology needs no philosophic support; nor is it, indeed, a science. Its purpose is purely practical and its truth is exalted far above human reason, for it rests on divine truth.[182] The fulfillment of the prophecies and the Old and New Testament miracles, the common agreement among the writers of the Bible (an argument which betrays the superficiality of our *"doctor subtilis"*), and the agreement of Bible teachings with the long-lasting Catholic Church—these are Duns Scotus' proofs of the truth of revelation.

As a consequence of his theory of will, for Scotus there is no good *per se;* no act is good in itself, but only because God has willed it. If God were to condone murder, murder would then be good.

Naturally, there can be no question of genuine criticism with Scotus. His polemics against Thomism did not spring from intellectual skepticism, but from devotion to dogma. With him Catholic dogma stood above and beyond mere knowledge.

ROGER BACON

The English Franciscan monk, Roger Bacon (1214-1294), brought out the true character of Scholasticism in picturesque fashion. He divided philosophy into "philosophy of faith" and "philosophy without faith." The former he subordinated to theology, while the latter he rejected as harmful and hellish.[183] Bacon conceived the purpose of philosophy to be the demonstration of the truth of the revealed teachings of the Gospels, Catholic dogma, and the duties of the Christian religion.[184]

He concluded that the Jewish patriarchs as well as the Christian Apostles were "true philosophers," who knew everything.[185] As proof of this, he pointed to the Biblical miracles performed by the patriarchs (as he put it) through their complete mastery of natural laws.

It is well to remember that Bacon was imprisoned for many years by the Catholic Church on the charge of witchcraft. Yet his inclinations toward experimentation were kept in sharp check by his faith in Aristotelian philosophy. He opposed both Albertus Magnus and Thomas Aquinas, calling them boys who had tried to teach before learning anything themselves, and would become doctors *"sine arte nulla artium magistri et sine doctrina doctores."*

However liberating Bacon's influence may appear to have been, and however sympathetic we may be to his battle with Albertus and Thomas, we must remember that he still personified Scholastic philosophy with its dogmatism, though in its best form. His philosophy likewise reveals the shocking ignorance of his period and the limited education available in schools dominated entirely by Catholic metaphysics.

WILLIAM OF OCKHAM

Another Franciscan, William of Ockham (died 1349), made himself conspicuous among the Scholastics by taking up the foolish battle of Roscellinus against the imaginary Ideas or universals.[186] He avoided the threat his theories raised to accepted Catholic dogmas, like the trinity and transubstantiation, by embracing Duns Scotus' dictum: "Something may be false philosophically but true theologically." Besides, William explained, wherever his teachings came into conflict with those of the Church, they were not to be taken seriously, but merely as part of a superficial method of training the mind![187]

This strikes one as even more peculiar since Ockham was so busy trying to subjugate the mind to faith. He praised faith precisely *because* it was not logical. Still cogent was Tertullian's famous statement, which had ruled Catholic philosophy for over a thousand years: *"Credo quia absurdum.* I believe because it is illogical."

RAYMOND LULLY

The Franciscan, Raymond Lully (1235-1315), who held salon at the court of the king of Majorca, was another of the singular individuals of those dark days. Lully had been driven into the arms of philosophy by an unfortunate love affair. He commenced the study of logic, but with typical light-headedness could not keep at it, so he devised a mystic alphabet to convince pagans of the truth of Catholicism. He had little success in Rome or at the Church councils, but he was permitted to dispute the articles of Christian faith in Mohammedan countries. In the end he was assassinated by an irritated opponent.

NICOLAUS CUSANUS

Nicolaus Cusanus, or Nicholas of Cusa (1401-1448), pope's legate and later cardinal, was no friend of the Scholastic method as practiced by the "rationalists." Inclined rather to a Platonizing philosophy, he was influenced by Erigena. In his major work, *Doctrine of Ignorance,* he attempted to show the weakness of natural reason, in order to defend the "conscious ignorance" of the faithful. His works, needless to say, earned wide popular acclaim. Some historians have called him a pantheist, but Cusanus considered the world a reflection of God, unquestionably created by Him.[187] His distinction between God, visible world and individual things is found later in Cartesian and clarified in Spinozaistic philosophy. Cardinal Cusanus conceded divine attributes to the Logos, but with limitations. For instance, whereas he called God "infinite," he called the Logos "without end"; and whereas God was "eternal," the Logos was "non-temporal." [188]

BONAVENTURA

In addition to those who sought intellectual satisfaction from theological speculations, there were others in the Scholastic period who allowed their emotions to prevail. And whereas the "rationalists" argued about the trinal existence of God, Platonic life after death and the Christian methods of attaining it, and bodily resurrection, proved by Aristotelian logic, the "emotionalists" chose a different jumping-off place to plunge into the same metaphysical waters.

Even Thomas Aquinas suffered from ecstasies in his old age. His visual and aural hallucinations caused his kinfolk to marvel, particularly when he declared, after an attack of "beatific vision," that all his works were as chaff in comparison with what he had just witnessed.

In the case of Bonaventura (1221-1274), the *"doctor*

seraphicus" who walked in the company of "the bride of the soul of Jesus," and enjoyed a foretaste of celestial bliss while yet in the vale of this world, these ecstasies were much stronger than with Aquinas. These "enlightenments of faith" gave the metaphysician more certainty than all natural knowledge. "How ignorant are the learned!" Bonaventura exclaimed. "They must err, for they have no faith." [189]

Scholasticism was not always opposed to mysticism; often it joined forces with it, as in the cases of Thomas and Bonaventura.

JOHN ECKHART

The German Dominican monk, John Eckhart (1260-1327), attained the highest peak among those "God-seers" who effected a direct union between the Catholic universal God and the soul-god which was Plotinus' legacy to Europe. "Common sense must be reckoned as naught since God was born" is the theme song of Eckhart and his followers, Tauler and Suso.

Here is a typical Eckhartian statement: "You should drown your ego and let your 'I' become the 'me' in his 'me,' that you may understand, together with Him, His uncreated being and His unnamed ego."

In his ecstasy, Eckhart differentiated between a naturalized and an unnaturalized godhead. When the spark, the essence of the soul, cleanses itself of sin, of all things and of itself (*cf.* Philo), then God is born within the soul.[190] The soul must accept Him with calm. By withdrawing from all things, man becomes God. The soul strives toward God, evades all sensation and attains a state of forgetfulness—forgetfulness even of self.[191]

In fact, Katrei of Strassburg, one of Eckhart's pupils, came to him one day and said, "Rejoice with me, Master, I have become God!" His claim was too much for the Catholic Church. Its leaders called the ecstatic preacher to account, but Eckhart protested fiercely his "horror at any mistake in faith."

Eckhartian mysticism found many adherents and imitators, without, however, slipping the bonds of Catholicism. Some religious philosophers have attempted to keep Eckhart's ideas alive even in our own day.

THE BEGINNING OF EXPERIMENTAL SCIENCE

Toward the end of the Middle Ages, the overbearing claims of the Catholic Church awakened an ever growing restlessness. The popes' constant struggles for secular power raised doubts among the wide masses about the sincerity of their teachings. Long before Martin Luther nailed his theses to the Wittenberg church door, the people were moving toward Protestantism. We know little of their silent protests, but of their articulate ones the Catholic executioners have left an original record.

Greek and Roman literature in non-Catholic dress was forcing its way into Europe, and wandering classical scholars were gradually invading the conservative Catholic institutions of learning. The development of the printing press toward the end of the fifteenth century and the discovery of far-distant lands previously unknown, pushed back the horizon of man's knowledge and stirred the ignorant to amazement and doubt.

The strengthened burgher classes turned their attention to the school system and began to favor other than Roman-trained teachers. As a consequence, the youth educated in these schools became freer and more inquiring in spirit. The gradual strengthening of the non-clerical classes in their half-conscious struggle for autonomy contributed inevitably to the reawakening and growth of the empirical spirit. The values of the much misunderstood Renaissance were not only literary.

Those who took the first steps in modern science did not imitate the old philosophic methods, but applied themselves to practical experiment and theory. The three towering personalities of the period were Copernicus, Kepler and Galileo. Upon these three our modern scientific method stands or falls. Opposing the whole medieval world with their passion for scientific search, they turned the benighted face of Europe toward the sun. Each was a teacher of independent investigation, a conqueror of theological confusion, and a champion of empirical science.

What attitude, then, did religious metaphysics take toward their experimental achievements? What influence did theology exert upon their work, and what benefit did it derive from their discoveries? The answer must be: Upon the pioneers of science philosophy had no influence whatever, and from their sincere investigations metaphysics learned precisely nothing!

What could Copernicus, whose gigantic work on the motion of the heavenly bodies smashed the idolized Aristotelian cosmology, learn from Aristotle? How could ancient philosophy help Kepler in his brand-new investigation into the form of light and its refraction? How could it assist him in the discovery of the three laws of motion of the planets? On the one hand, we have the exact experiments of a scholar who laid the foundations of astronomy and optics; on the other, a sea of fanciful notions about transcendent essences and substances. And did Thomas Aquinas guide Galileo in the discovery of the laws of falling bodies, inclined planes and the pendulum? For Plato physics was nothing; for Aristotle, little more. Their ideas floated serenely beyond and outside of nature. Yet from their time to the time of Galileo, no greater philosophers had existed. What, then, could these metaphysicians and their imitators teach the founders of physics?

Galileo appreciated the threat of metaphysics as no one before or after him. This appreciation lay at the bottom of his inexorable struggle with the Aristotelian method. He wrote bitterly to Kepler of seeing "the professor of philosophy at Pisa labor with philosophic arguments before the duke as if it were possible to derive new planets out of the heavens by magic formula!"

Aristotle had argued that the moon is smooth and bright; with his telescope Galileo discovered the opposite to be true. Aristotle theorized that the heavier a body is, the faster it falls to the earth. By dropping objects of different weight from the tower of Pisa, Galileo demonstrated the law of equality of acceleration of motion. Aristotle conceived that all planets revolve about the earth. Galileo observed four planets moving around Jupiter and proved the falsity of the philosopher's assumption.

Yet the times were so chained by philosophy that people had greater confidence in the dead letter than in their living senses. When Galileo announced his discovery of sunspots, a philosopher wrote him: "I have searched all the works of Aristotle and have found no reference to sunspots. Be assured, therefore, that it is a delusion, either of your eyes or of your glasses."

How wonderfully William Gilbert, the discoverer of magnetic force, has expressed it. "In the discovery of the unknown, and in the investigation of the unknown causes of phenomena, clear proof of reliable experiments is given, not the speculations and desires of the professors and philosophers." Who knows where we of the twentieth century might be had not such men as Copernicus, Kepler and Galileo cast off the chains of theology? And who knows where we might be if scientific method had been established two and a half millennia ago?

The fact is that in two thousand years of undisputed reign, from Thales to Cusanus, metaphysics accomplished virtually nothing productive: physics and astronomy built on fables, medicine and chemistry at the mercy of ignorance and superstition, politics and pedagogy in the hands of narrow-minded religious bigots. During the entire period of theological domination, Europe remained in an unaltered state of scientific sterility.

In the few hundred years since the liberation of science

from theology, a totally new era has come to Europe. It might be more appropriate to begin our calendar with the Copernican revolution rather than with the birth of any of the Hebrew or Moslem prophets.

There is the time before Copernicus and the time after Copernicus. The theological world and the scientific world. Copernicus stands at the turning point in Western culture.

Metaphysical speculation by no means died out with the birth of modern science. While the physicists and biologists, mathematicians and astronomers, physicians and chemists, and other scholars pursued their labors, unearthing the secrets of nature, the metaphysicians squatted down in the road of tradition, unperturbed by the gigantic strides being taken all around them, and continued to dispute whether an eel is really an eel or an egg, an egg.

We shall now observe the curious route taken by philosophy after the birth of modern science. It will then become obvious that metaphysics has a most peculiar place within the realm of scientific investigation.

JAKOB BOHME

There is no unity of opinion regarding the fatherhood of modern speculative philosophy. Three metaphysicians contend for the title: the German shoemaker, Jakob Böhme; the Italian poet, Giordano Bruno; and the French mathematician, René Descartes.

By his own confession, Jakob Böhme (1575-1624), a shoemaker of Görlitz, in his boyhood suffered from hallucinations which recurred in later years. He relates how he had wandered for seven days in the celestial realm of divine happiness and was able to give a minute description of his experiences there. The sight of a tin vessel brought him to the very *"centro"* of nature's secrets. This revelation did not come to him, however, until his head had been turned by the formulas of the theosophists, theologists and astrologers (Paracelsus).[192] Moreover, Böhme had a weakness

90

for the esoteric writings which were anything but scarce in his century; he gave full play to his love of the obscure in a cryptic, florid language.

Thus it is difficult for us to discern any system or even plain meaning in the enigmatic style of the pious shoemaker. The essence of his philosophy seems to be a fanatic belief in the three principles of God. That is to say, God expressed Himself under three aspects: the kingdom of hell where the Devil rages as executioner, the kingdom of heaven where the heart of God soothes His wrath, and finally the world of earth.[193] Leaving out the earth, we are confronted with the familiar Biblical landscapes of heaven and hell, which, according to the Apocalypse, emanate from the Father, the Son and the Holy Ghost, and are each divided into three parts, plus a mediary substance, fire. The blame for this splintering of God lies, of course, with Lucifer, who brought it about.[194]

It is entirely in man's hands whether he goes to the heavenly kingdom or to hell. After death the soul cannot change its fate, which has been determined in this world.[195] And while bad souls are tortured by evil spirits in the chambers of suffering, good souls fly blissfully heavenward without the remotest concern for those delivered to the Devil; that problem is left to the angels who are engaged in constant war with him. On the day of resurrection, the good souls will be rewarded with bliss, while the evil souls and devils will be punished.[196]

In accounting for the creation, Böhme leans on both the Torah and the famous astrologer, alchemist and miracle-worker, Bombastus Paracelsus (ca. 1493-1541). Earth was originally part of "the eternal saltpeter," but upon the fall of Lucifer was vomited forth because it was too hard. On the third day of creation, the fire of lightning awakened the seven spirits also imprisoned in the saltpeter, and they in turn called the herbs and plants to life. Therefore each plant has seven qualities; likewise in the purification of metals seven meltings are necessary, one for each quality. The powers of the seven spirits are invested in the stars; in each

91

planet a different quality is discernible.[197] The task of these spirits is the creation of man. Accordingly, our life springs from the power of the sun and planets; and the elements bring a child to life, nourish it throughout its existence, bringing it fortune or misfortune and, ultimately, death.[198]

Böhme has a clear kinship with older mystic systems. His search for a "primal ground," "the kingdom of light," and other abstract beings force one to relate him to Cabbalistic writings.[199]

GIORDANO BRUNO

Giordano Bruno of Nola (1548-1600) spent his early years in the various cloisters of the Dominican order, including one greatly influenced by Thomas Aquinas. But the young man's dislike of asceticism and penance eventually brought him into conflict with his superiors, and Brother Bruno was obliged to seek refuge in distant lands. Having studied philosophy à la Raymond Lully and Nicolaus Cusanus, he earned his livelihood during his exile by teaching. He specialized in the dubious art of mnemonics and the mysterious Lullian one of solving philosophic problems by manipulating concentric circles inscribed with philosophic concepts. His skill in this led many to suspect him of witchcraft. He also believed in palmistry, in the swearing of the dead, in the healing power of precious stones and magic roots, and in other superstitions of a like kind.[200]

His theological dissent and an inexpungible hatred of the Aristotelian-Thomistic Dominicans gave Bruno no peace. His restless wandering took him through Northern Italy into Calvinistic Geneva. From there he visited France and England, where he composed a series of philosophic pamphlets, and then proceeded to Germany. There he remained, writing poetry and philosophy, until one of his disciples made the unfortunate suggestion that he return to Italy. In that country he was immediately seized and hauled before the Inquisitorial tribune. When he refused to recant his heretical views, he was condemned by the Church, practicing the well known brand of brotherly love and forbearance (as the verdict said, *"citra sanguinis effusionem"*), to be burned alive.

The poet Giordano Bruno is one of the most sympathetic figures in the history of philosophy. He borrowed many of his views from Neoplatonic writings which he mistakenly ascribed to Pythagoras and Empedocles. He put great faith in ibn-Gabirol. He was imbued with enthusiasm for "the infinite," "the one" that penetrates all being and inspires it, the "world-soul" that is the cause and ruler of all existence.[201]

Bruno's works show that it is a mistake to call Bruno a pure pantheist.[202] All his life he remained a true Catholic and never joined any of the Protestant reform sects that admired him. To the end he strove to return to the fold of the Mother Church. In 1586 he tried, through the intervention of the papal nuncio, to be accepted back into the Church, and his ultimate desire was to be awarded a priesthood outside the Dominican order through a clear presentation of his philosophy to the Pope.

In spite of his poetry and classical learning, it is the personal God who emerges from Bruno's philosophy,[203] the God who had made Rome His capital, the God of the faithful and the superstitious. Yet there was this difference: Bruno was ready to die for his God, while others contrived to make an excellent living out of Him.

FRANCIS BACON

Before we proceed to Descartes, we should mention a shrewd English lawyer who raised quite a stir in his day and impressed many as a leader of men. This was Francis Bacon (1561-1626), who by ingenious intrigues and tricky stratagems elevated himself to the lordship of the Privy Seal, the chancellorship, lordship of Verulam and viscountship of St. Albans. Bacon unscrupulously sacrificed his friend and protector, Lord Essex, in order to retain the favor of the queen. But when, upon the accession of James I, the party of Essex returned to power, Bacon was among the first to hail the executed lord.

Bacon's treachery is too well known to be rehearsed here. It was brought to an abrupt end by the parliamentary investigation of 1621, by which time Bacon had raised himself to the top rung of the political ladder. The Lord of the Privy Seal was found guilty of corruption and bribery, and was condemned to hard labor in prison, loss of citizenship rights, and exile from London.[204]

Having made a name for himself as an essayist in his youth, Francis Bacon wrote a number of philosophic works both before and during his exile. To his first philosophic piece he gave the somewhat pretentious title of *The Great Birth of Time*. Bacon felt himself peculiarly fitted to advocate the restoration of the sciences, though he had dabbled in them but slightly—in some, mathematics and astronomy, for instance, not at all. He failed to recognize the great scientists and inventors of his age, but perpetuated a great deal of medieval superstition and played around with all kinds of childish experiments. His condemnation of Aristotelian and Platonic philosophy signifies little; to do so was the fashion in the England of his time. His struggle against the dogmatism of the ancients is invalidated by his own dogmatism. There is much shallow conversationalism in Bacon, and little consequence.

Bacon divided philosophy into three parts: physics, metaphysics and theology. His inclusion of physics and theology in philosophy shows a regression into the Aristotelianism he professed to reject, and his search for end causes (*"causae finales"*) in addition to natural causes (*"causae efficientes"*) links him with Platonism. At every point, this champion of a divided philosophy indicates that "the full flower of philosophy is religion."

But let us not take these phrases of Bacon too seriously; they have been taken so too often. Let us merely note that his ethical and social principles, whose highest expression is the preference of social benefits over individual integrity, have found only too widespread acceptance.

RENE DESCARTES

Whereas Francis Bacon pleaded for a regeneration of the sciences, yet ignored the scientists of his age, the French philosopher, René Descartes du Perron (1596-1650), was a mathematician of note and consequence. A volunteer soldier in many armies, Descartes spent most of his spare time and unquestionable abilities on problems which may have seemed important to him, but which are sometimes little more than the playful games of a scholarly dilettante. Unable to forget his Jesuit upbringing and prompted by his enthusiastic friends, he overreached himself in an attempt to write a new "natural philosophy." Still bogged down in the old swamps of metaphysics, he threw himself into a whole series of sciences. Eventually the solid practical achievements of his contemporaries led him to realize the futility of his undertaking, and he returned to his first love, mathematics.

Upon the urging of his friends, Descartes began to set down his philosophic ideas in writing. For a long time his natural timidity and fear of the Catholic Church, which he greatly honored, kept him from making these ideas public. For the same reason he refrained from setting down his ethical theories.[205] It is for the rulers, he said, to prescribe laws of conduct. He insisted that Catholic theology could be combined with his philosophy, and tried to base his ideas on the Biblical story of creation and on Biblical genealogy.[206] "The main problem of my metaphysical tract," he wrote his friend Mersennes, "is to prove the existence of God and the life of the soul after it has departed from the body. I burn with anger when I see that there are men who, bold and shameless, feel themselves worthy of contending with God." [207]

For Descartes, the existence of the trinal Catholic Deity

was the main theme of philosophy. He directed his prayers for enlightenment to the Virgin Mother of God, and even made a pilgrimage to the sepulcher of Mary at Loreto.[208] "Never," he declared, "will a treatise come into the world from my pen in which there would be the slightest word that could be disapproved of by the Church." And when the condemnation of Galileo was rumored, Descartes burned his *Cosmos*, fearful that it might not be Catholic enough. Yet he claimed, "I think I have discovered how metaphysical truth can be demonstrated with as much certainty as the principles of geometry."

Starting from the fundamental principle of all science, *"De omnibus dubitandum,"* Descartes elaborated the rational method which was to dominate European thought for more than a century. Like St. Augustine, he asked, "What is certain?" "My first and only certainty," he answered, "lies in my thought. *Cogito ergo sum*—I think, therefore I am." With this fundamental Augustinian principle Descartes ended the first part of his introspective philosophy. Continuing his Catholic reasoning (this time à la Thomas Aquinas), Descartes argued, "I have an idea of God as an infinite being, but I, as a finite being, cannot produce from within myself an idea of the infinite. Thus an infinite and perfect divinity must exist outside of me." [209] But the meditations of Descartes go further than the ontological proof of the existence of God. He wanted a criterion for the universal validity of truth. Therefore he concluded: "God is not a liar, therefore all that I see clearly and distinctly is necessarily true." [210] But truer than truth itself are the revelations and decisions of the Church councils, for Catholic theology stands as far above philosophy as revelation is above human reason.[211]

"All change is a sign of shortcoming. God, as a perfect substance, has no shortcomings; therefore God can never change." [212] This is a typical example of a Cartesian argument. Or again: God is thinking substance. But he is incorporeal, for body implies divisibility and divisibility means imperfection; therefore God is infinite and incorporeal, a thinking being but without sense perception.[213]

After the foregoing, we can perhaps better understand the German philosopher who said he did not feel in the least speculative while attending the lectures of Descartes.

At first, Descartes posited God as the one idea inborn in man, while all other ideas were acquired. Later, he added other "inborn" ideas, such as the idea of the soul, of mathematics, of color, and so on. Finally he comes to the conclusion that all ideas are innate.[214]

The notion of clarity as a criterion of truth is as old as Stoic philosophy, but it did not always have the Catholic color Descartes gave it. The thought that the idea of God is inborn was also several thousand years older than Descartes.[215]

We mention these points as evidence of the lack of originality in modern philosophy. Limited in its resources, it often reached back into antiquity, to draw its concepts from prescientific, religious eras. With the rise of the empirical method, philosophy had no field of action left to it. When the sciences deserted it, there was no longer the same urgency to keep it vital and creative. At the beginning of the modern era, philosophy lost its very justification for existence.

The mathematics of Descartes is imposing; his philosophy severely limited. Like many who followed him, Descartes could never free himself completely from traditional metaphysics. How much more might he have accomplished for science, had philosophy held no charms for him. Indeed, the famous steps of his method (intuition, analysis, synthesis, and review) are essentially those of the modern scientist. In Descartes we have one of those rare instances where knowledge and superstition, science and philosophy, are combined in the same individual.

It is worth noting that in his earlier writings on the methods of logic (*deductio* or *inductio*), Descartes, in true Platonic fashion, favored the intuitive method (*intuitio*).[216] In defining intuition, he resorts to some very vague terms.

97

As to its source, he knew as much or as little as the recent champion of this mystic system of thought, Henri Bergson. One belief does emerge clearly from the philosophy of Descartes: It is not the mind but the will that accomplishes the act of judgment.

The psychology of Descartes is a storehouse of human error. At the time when Harvey was discovering the circulation of the blood and laying the foundations of modern medicine, Descartes was philosophizing about "dust-like living spirits" which come in contact with the nerves and so "mediate between the perceptions and motion." The soul has its seat in the *glans pinealis,* which is in the center of the brain, and from which it sends out its commands to all parts of the body. Man is a "machine inspired by life spirits." [217]

Metaphysicians of the last century wrestled long and vainly with the problem of how the Cartesian soul affected the body and was in turn affected by it.

According to Descartes, animals are without consciences or feelings; they are mere eating and drinking machines.[218]

What Descartes accomplished philosophically was to express the Scholastic ideas of substance in mathematical formulas. Relying on Cardinal Cusanus, he distinguished between a thinking substance and a body substance in addition to the substance of God. The substance of God needs nothing outside itself for its existence, but the substance of thought and body require the substance of God for their existence.[219] This idea became a major theme in modern philosophy and is one of the reasons Descartes is known as "the founder of modern metaphysics."

BARUCH SPINOZA

Among the hundreds of men of greater or less importance in the history of philosophy, Baruch Spinoza (1632-1677) holds a unique position. Abhorred and reviled for more than a hundred years by the intellectual elite of

Europe, this so-called wicked little atheist had, by the end of the eighteenth century, become a symbol of sanctity. Great men like Herder, Goethe and Lessing revered this strange man and his original ideas, and as the decades went by, the light of Baruch Spinoza's brilliant thought shone brighter and brighter.

No man can be fully understood without an adequate knowledge of his background; and if Spinoza seems to be an enigmatic figure, so were his epoch and his environment.

Spinoza was the descendant of a Jewish family which had been driven from Spain by the Inquisition, first to Portugal, then to Holland. The latter country offered only a partial refuge, for in the seventeenth century Holland had its own brands of religious and political persecution. Young Spinoza found little happiness in his step-mother's house in Amsterdam, and we hear of him as an adolescent frequently wandering away from the Spanish-speaking "ghetto," to mingle with his Christian neighbors. Amsterdam was at that time seething with Socinians, Quakers and other reformist sects, a situation which helped the young student of the Torah and the Talmud to approach Scripture with an amazingly analytical and objective eye.

By his detached viewpoint, the young Spinoza brought to light indisputable discrepancies between various sections of the Canon, and confronted scholars with disturbing evidence that some of the traditionally ancient writings had been composed only a few hundred years B.C., and by entirely different hands than the orthodoxy alleged. This was the beginning of modern theological exegetics or Biblical criticism. The Jewish community of Amsterdam, most of whose members had suffered harrowing tortures at the hands of the Catholic Church, made desperate efforts to stop Spinoza from proselytizing among their people. What they especially feared was Spinoza's thesis that the laws of the Torah were state laws designed for the tribes of Israel, and therefore had no validity for Jews living in other states. If this interpretation were accepted, it would mean the dissolution of those religious ties by which the Torah had for thousands of years held together Jews scattered to the four corners of the earth. When pleas and threats proved to be of no avail, the twenty-four-year-old Spinoza was officially expelled from the Jewish community of Amsterdam. He spent the remainder of his life in other Dutch towns, mostly in and around The Hague.

Immediately after his excommunication, Spinoza had published in Spanish a pamphlet entitled *Apologia,* which explained his position. Until this day not one copy of the pamphlet has been discovered, though many years later, in the only book published during his lifetime, *The Theological Political Treatise,* he expounded his point of view in great detail. His main thesis is an appeal to reason, with the recommendation that the secular powers of the Church be curbed, so that every man may be granted full liberty of thought and speech.

In his philosophic mind, Spinoza is a student of Descartes, but in his findings he ranges far afield from the French mathematician. In his *Ethics,* which is designed after Euclid's Geometry, he begins with a number of what he considers irrefutable premises, on which he builds a system analyzing the nature of God and man in a purely scientific manner. He identifies God with creative nature, and with substance. Mortal man knows only two attributes, the world of the body and the world of the mind; but God (or substance) lives through infinite attributes, each of which in turn necessarily expresses eternal and infinite essentiality.

This majestic concept of our mind-body universe, as, so to speak, only a splinter in eternity, has had a profound effect upon physicists and scholars from Leibniz to Einstein. Man himself, Spinoza reasons, is like all things a part, a mode, of created nature and must be taken as such and no more. Like other things, he is constantly in motion and has no free will of his own. He is filled with contradictory emotions of fear and hope, love and hate, pity and remorse. The only path to freedom from such an embattled existence is to be overwhelmed by an even greater emotion: the love of God, which is, indeed, the same as the love of man. Love of God is born out of deep understanding of the nature of the universe, and it is given only to those who perceive intellectually the self-identical order of ideas and things as attributes of the all-pervading One. Whoever gains this high intuition will become imbued with *amor dei intellectualis,* the rational love of God.

Thus the man who understands the order of creative nature, through his feeling of inner blessedness, sloughs off the disturbing passions of ambition, greed and lust, to enjoy the constant pleasure of fulfillment in having reached the life of adequate cognition. The highest good is therefore knowledge of God, and to know God is to enjoy the most nearly perfect happiness; while to entertain inadequate ideas is to give oneself over to the passions. The pleasure of blessedness so far exceeds the pleasure offered by the passions, that the truly self-seeking person will strive toward the understanding of God and cling to it. Only the emotion born of intuition and reason can conquer the petty appetites of daily life and keep those few who attain it, free and wise and secure.

Spinoza, the moralist, attacks the problems of human conduct with the same weapon he uses in theological matters, namely, pure reason. Experience teaches, he maintains, that man is subject to three basic passions: the passion for gold, the passion for honor, and the sex passion. As long as man is beset by any of these three, he is not his own master, but resembles a rudderless ship floundering in a sea of greeds. It is interesting to note that Spinoza does not speak of the libidinous nature of man as "immoral." By his standard, there is nothing in nature good or bad, evil or virtuous of itself. Things become good or bad only in relation to a third value. This value is Spinoza's concept of the quietude of the soul. Since he considers this quietude the greatest blessing and the *summum bonum* of being, whatever keeps man from attaining it is negative, or bad, while whatever helps him reach this state of supreme happiness is positive, or good. Since reason is the only means by which man can master his raging passions, Spinoza considers their conquest an intellectual process.

To him, then, the wise man is *eo ipso* the free man, who no longer is pulled in every direction by greed, lust or ambition, but who, rather, in full consciousness of his inner self and his unity with the All, leads a life of spiritual independence and serenity. To reach such a rarefied state is, admittedly, an arduous task, possible to only a few select minds. But then, Spinoza reminds us, all things of grandeur are as rare as they are difficult.

THE CABBALA

The literature of the Cabbala presents a peculiar mixture of Neopythagorean, Neoplatonic and Jewish ideas, brought together without order or form in the books called *Yezira* (700-900) and *Zohar* (1300-1500). In addition to these are numerous works and fragments of works of Cabbalistic content, filled with subtle religious fancies. The belief in amulets, magic formulas for the revival of dead love, incantations for the lulling of storms can all be found in this philosophy.[220] The authors of *Yezira* and *Zohar* are unknown. Ibn-Gabirol and others traced the *Sefer Yezira* back to the patriarch Abraham. Still others have ascribed it to Adam, the first man. The *Zohar* contains internal evidence pointing to Rabbi Moses de Leon (1250-1305) as the possible author.

The two masterpieces of the Cabbala expound a metaphysics based on the twenty-two letters of the Hebrew alphabet. The first ten letters of the alphabet stand for categories of being. The *Zohar* contains also the Pythagorean theory of the transmigration of souls, as well as a theory of emanation of the female and son principle which led to the association of the Cabbala with the Christian concept of the trinity.

The Cabbala reached its high point in the widely known miracle-worker and herald of the Messiah, Rabbi Isaac

Luria (1534-1572), whose ecstatic revelations have been preserved in writing, along with the visions of his pupil, Hayyim Vital. By the seventeenth century Cabbalistic mysticism had reached such a point that a sly Smyrnean, Sabbatai Zevi, proclaimed himself the Messiah in the prescribed way. Only his subsequent conversion to Mohammedanism put an end to his golden opportunity. From then on, the Cabbala began to lose ground, though remnants of this mystic philosophy have been kept alive to this day among small groups of Eastern European Jews. Among later metaphysicians, Jakob Böhme concerned himself seriously with the Cabbala.

THOMAS HOBBES

The vagueness of metaphysical speculation made itself felt in political and judicial theory no less than in the other sciences. We find even modern thinkers preaching the ancient idealism. This idealism, deduced from metaphysical axioms of long standing, almost invariably goes contrary to the interests of the common people. Curiously enough, these political and judicial metaphysicians hide their assumptions behind the articles of faith of the enemies of freedom.

The English Thomas Hobbes (1588-1679), a tutor in the homes of lords whose power was on the wane in the great struggle between rulers and people in Western Europe, was one of these backward-looking political philosophers. At the time of the struggle between the independents and royalists, Hobbes, a middle-class ornament of the English court, placed himself on the safe side by charging the people with disobedience to the king, whose rights he supported by quotations from the Scriptures.

Hobbes asserted: "All power comes from God and, where there is a ruler, he has been placed in his position by God. Wherefore, whoever offers resistance to the ruling powers offers resistance to God." And further: "God Himself wrote in the Bible of the right of kings: he will take

103

your sons into his army, he will take your daughters to serve him, he will take your best olive fields and distribute them among his servants." [221]

Every opposition to the king is an unpardonable sin. As God-ordained ruler, the royal monarch has full authority over his subjects and total power over their wealth and faith.[222] Besides all this, continued Hobbes, "The revolutionary is stupid for of every twenty rebels only one achieves the laurel. All the others are killed." [223] Hobbes neglected to state that the rebel might be driven by forces other than personal greed and thirst for honor.

This philosophy mocking all human rights aroused considerable opposition, intensified by its author's vanity in describing himself as the creator of *philosophia civilis,* and comparing himself to Copernicus, Galileo and Harvey. Eventually Hobbes was driven out of England. He wrote sorrowfully of the disobedient people who had rejected his gospel: "I have been long of the opinion that a wise statesman can never please the people, and that the masses cannot understand a wisdom which surpasses their understanding." [224]

But why should the English people have listened to the hoarse whisper of a philosopher who urged them to love slavery because it was the rule of nature, to worship tyranny because it was a divine institution—at the very time Oliver Cromwell was crying, "Let us put to shame the insane notion that the people belong to the king and the church to the pope"?

The fact that Hobbes went over to Cromwell after the fall of the monarchy, and returned to the king when the crown was restored—that he evidently wanted to serve only the reigning party with his pen—throws considerable light on his motivations.[225]

NICOLAS MALEBRANCHE

Nicolas Malebranche (1638-1715), who, like the Dutch Arnold Geulincx (1625-1669), tried to prove Christian dogma by Cartesian philosophy, was a contemporary of Spinoza. "That part of metaphysics is most useful to us," he said, "that offers us clear and simple proof of the dogmas; therefore metaphysics may be said to serve religion." [226] Malebranche was of the further opinion that in all things that are beyond our understanding we should subordinate reason to faith. To tackle such problems rationally is dangerous and detrimental.[227] Although, in the fashion of his day, Malebranche called for a mathematical presentation of science, philosophy and theology, like Spinoza he clothed his philosophy in religious metaphors. To the saints alone he granted an intuitive knowledge of truth in this world; to ordinary men such intuition comes only in the afterworld.[228]

Under the influence of Saint Augustine, Malebranche said he hoped "to acquire insight and wisdom through faith." [229] Thus does philosophy move in circles, ever returning to the old, familiar paths. Even here, at the beginning of the eighteenth century, we have gone back to the old proposition: "I believe in order that I may understand."

Malebranche is as vague as Geulincx regarding God's relation to the world. At one time God is identical with nature; at another He stands above nature. At one moment he explains that everything proceeds in its natural order according to the laws of creation; at another, that God Himself ordains the least event. But on one point both rationalists agree: All things are in God and we see all things in Him.[230] This notion, of course, is as vague as the notion of the capricious interference of God in man's actions.

The Christian pantheist, as Malebranche is lovingly called, offered a most meaningful explanation of the aim of this world: God made the world in order to have something to play with! [231] This notion made such a deep impression on Fichte that he contrived many variations on the same tune.

GOTTFRIED WILHELM LEIBNIZ

In addition to his mathematical and historical studies, the diplomat, Gottfried Wilhelm Leibniz (1646-1716), busied himself also with philosophy. Characteristically, he wanted above everything to harmonize all ideas and make all knowledge agree. He boasted that he had found some truth in every philosopher, which he had incorporated into his own system. He called himself "Placidus" ("Peacemaker"). However well he realized his aim, this much is certain: Leibniz borrowed practically all his ideas from earlier philosophers. "My theory of substance," he wrote, "is identical with that of the Aristotelian school, except that they failed to recognize the 'monads.'"[232] On another occasion, he compared his theory of substance with that of Spinoza.

The principle of "monads" in Leibniz' philosophy can be traced back more than two thousand years to the atomic theory of Leucippus and the mathematical monads (units) of Pythagoras. Nor do Leibniz' monads appear much different from the Ideas of Plato. These monads, though they do not expand (a fact which does not keep them from being so distant from each other that no two are alike), are the basic molecules of nature.[233] Leibniz evades the question whether the monads are material or transcend the material by saying that they are "well-founded phenomena" *(phénomène bien fondé)*. When the occasion suits him, he identifies them with the soul and contrasts them with the body *(natura secunda)*.[234] All monads have consciences. No monad, however, affects another. The monads have no windows looking outward.[235]

Leibniz has his own conception of the relation of body and soul. This relationship is so contrived "that the body works as if it had no soul, and the soul, as if it had no body; but at the same time they work as if they affected each other."[236] When, for instance, a person recalls a tragic occurrence and tears fall from his eyes, it is not, according to Leibniz, the sad reminiscence which causes the tears.

Rather, God has so arranged it that at the precise moment of the sad memory tears fall independently. Leibniz makes wonderful use of this theory of pre-established divine harmony (previously enunciated by Geulincx—though Geulincx preferred to have God interfere in the pre-established harmony from time to time).[237]

Leibniz asserts quite plainly: "I state very sincerely that God was moved to create the world by a free emotion of kindness, and I conclude therefrom that this same emotion led him to create the best possible world." [238] With Scholastic lack of humor, Leibniz derives the existence of God from the necessity of the existence of "a perfect, unlimited being." He assures us that he can escape to such a God when natural causality does not suffice for him.[239]

In his theology, Leibniz tries to demonstrate how good and wise everything really is and that this is indeed the best of all possible worlds. The good in the world far outweighs the evil; indeed, there is really no evil, merely an absence of good. Suffering is necessary in order that we may appreciate happiness by contrast. As for sin, Leibniz assures us that in the other world there is a balanced system of justice. God can do no evil; if there is any in the world, God did not create it, but merely permitted it to come to be. With cosmic formulas of this sort Leibniz tries to unravel all metaphysical tangles.[240]

CHRISTIAN WOLFF

Christian Wolff of Breslau (1679-1754), a learned pupil of Leibniz, gathered the scattered ideas of his master into a single system, classified according to categories and properly titled. In the process, he introduced an endless number of time-honored terms, to give his synthesis a look of historic authenticity and impressiveness.

The entire Leibniz-Wolffian system, which for a brief time dominated the whole of cultural Germany, is in fact little more than a musty museum packed with ancient theological and philosophic dogmas, meaningless for the sciences, worthless for social life.

JOHN LOCKE

The English scholar, John Locke (1632-1704), exerted a quite beneficial influence on the cultural life of the seventeenth and eighteenth centuries. As a pioneer of natural pedagogy for the individual, he achieved noteworthy beginnings in modern methods of education. His espousal of the ideas of the revolutionary French earned him a wide reading public. In the political field Locke worked constantly for the liberation of the people from royal absolutism. Although he was still partially caught in the meshes of religious and metaphysical superstition, he contributed much to the return of human thought to a healthy, realistic foundation.

It was in his famous *Essay Concerning Human Understanding* that he perpetuated, *ad absurdum,* the old superstition of innate and eternal ideas which Descartes had accepted. The old Platonisms about eternal Ideas—of God, soul, freedom, substance, etc., etc.,—had perverted inquiry into human understanding for so long that Locke's immediate followers considered his views too materialistic. Reluctant to give up the old metaphysical speculations, they returned to the paths of Platonic speculation. For this Locke himself is partly to blame, for like his successors he dared not make a complete break with the past, but allowed his philosophy to be weakened by ideas which offered his opponents ready points of attack.

DAVID HUME

David Hume, the Scotch historian (1711-1776), scourged the theological and metaphysical speculations of philosophers. By showing the mechanical nature of the association of ideas, he gained great recognition in the field of experimental psychology. In fact, experimental psychology, which has struggled so valiantly in this century to free itself from the yoke of metaphysical psychology and logic, can point to no greater leaders than Locke and Hume. Idealist philosophy made every effort to shove these two thinkers into the background as materialists and skeptics. The critical spirit of the Enlightenment must have seemed sheer degeneracy to traditional philosophy, but we have come to realize that it was the path-clearer and vanguard in every realm of science.

GEORGE BERKELEY

The Irish bishop, George Berkeley (1685-1753), expounded a God-wedded, world-denying philosophy. Leaping back to Platonic poetry, Berkeley declared the world and all matter were merely imaginary (*esse-percipi*), owing their existence to the fact that they are ideas in the mind of God. Aside from these ideas, there is no reality; so-called "things" appear real only because God "thinks" them. Berkeley philosophized further that the equality of all objects can be traced to the impartiality of God. He declared all empirical investigation useless, since God can at any time change the nature of things.

It is obvious that Berkeley aligned himself strictly with the forces of orthodoxy and against the representatives of the Enlightenment. His idealism contributed heavily to the continued reactionary tone of European cultural life.

THE AGE OF ENLIGHTENMENT

In the eighteenth century, philosophy and religion fell upon hard times. The success of the scientists and explorers of the preceding century, and the daring propaganda of liberty-loving students of social science, had begun to undermine the ancient foundations of metaphysics. In the face of the century's impressive scientific achievements, the adherents of the old metaphysics ignored the temptation to fashion new theories in order to devote themselves to defending such traditional ideas as might still carry weight with their opponents. In truth, the unfruitful academic Scholasticism continued to flower almost everywhere, while the new shoots of empiricism grew only in obscure corners; but at least the scythe had been forged which was eventually to cut down the desiccated plants.

The eighteenth century, the century of the great liberators, ruthlessly sought to destroy every vestige of religio-metaphysical speculation. Men like Hume, Voltaire, Rousseau, Condillac, La Méttrie, Toland, Collins, Tyndale—a whole army of intellectual giants—joined the fight against superstition. In its battle for life, superstition raised the familiar cry for tolerance which the revolutionaries themselves had used against the merciless wielders of dogmatism. The intolerant superstition which had cast thousands upon the pyre for the sake of a word, now sought protection in a tolerance it had never itself exhibited.

But the ignorance which still reigned among the masses, still dominated by the forces of conservatism, prevented the spirit of an aroused Europe from using the victory in its hands. Religious dogmatism and metaphysical phantasy eventually resumed their authority. After the destructive attacks on metaphysics by Locke and Hume and the others, the renaissance of traditional philosophy was accomplished by professor Immanual Kant.

This final epoch of philosophy is all the more shameful because of the great and marvelous discoveries which the sciences were unfolding during the same time. One would suppose, after all that the human mind had discovered, invented and made available for the progress of man, that speculative philosophy and religion would have become a thing of the past. But no, they continue to weigh just as heavily on the society of our time.

110

IMMANUEL KANT

Professor Immanuel Kant (1724-1804) undertook the bold, but not really novel, task of forcing the world to recognize that the human mind cannot grasp things as they really are, but only as the mind conceives them.[241] He considered this discovery as important as Copernicus' discovery of the rotation of the earth—important because it supported "the desired possibility of a priori knowledge which should give us some knowledge of things before they are given us by perception."

With Aristotelian thoroughness, Kant engaged in an analysis of the categories in the soul and investigated (with peculiar partiality for the number twelve) aesthetic concepts and concepts of religion and judgment according to quantity, quality, modality and relation. With deep seriousness, he emptied the Wolffian well of its verbal wisdom, and where Wolff's ingenuity faltered, Kant enriched the philosophic vocabulary of the German language by borrowing from Greek, Latin and Hebrew. One may find in his works such words as "amphiboles," "antinomies," "Kathartikon," "noumena," "epigenesis," and so on.

According to Kant, each part of the soul has its own a priori inventory. He assumes that we will understand what he means by "a priori." It closely resembles Descartes' idea of "inherence," and stands as a contrast to the "a posteriori" knowledge of experience.

Reason possesses two a priori concepts, those of time and space. According to Kant, things are not near each other, nor do material events take place one after the other —that is only a deceptive appearance. The truth, rather, is that time and space are merely forms of the apperception of the understanding. Things do not really exist; it is our a priori concept of them which calls them into being. To convince the reader, Kant advises him to banish all objects from his thoughts. What then remains? Space, Kant answers. Of course, this is untrue. It is impossible for us to do away with things from our minds, and just as impossible to think "a priori." Kant concludes: A man cannot conceive of the nonexistence of space. Therefore, it is a priori! That is to say, because we see things in spatial relation to one another, space must have existed before we saw the objects in it. We might mention, at this point, Kant's efforts "to decide a priori, on the basis of inherent ideas, whether the moon has any effect on the weather or not."

Aristotle declared that the reason operates according to the general concepts of quantity, quality, relation, substance, space (place and position), time and causality (action and duration). Kant's fondness for the number twelve prompted him to expand Aristotle's categories to that number. He selected four of these and subordinated two others to each of the four. These categories, plus other a priori ideas, make up the basis of the transcendental being in man. According to Kant, the position of an object exists before the object, and its negation comes into existence before the thing itself. And if two things have a certain relationship in space, this relationship existed before the things themselves. Kant's a priori categories are causality, time and space.

Only the metaphysics of Aristotle can enable us to understand whence Kant derived his "ideas of pure reason," like God, soul, and the rest. When we come to the question of the effect of these a priori parts of the a priori soul, Kant becomes timid and takes refuge in Locke's statement that we can know nothing of the primary qualities of things, and that the essence of matter must remain a secret. Schopenhauer called Kant's distinction between noumena (things in themselves) and phenomena (the appearance of things) his greatest achievement, but this distinction is no more than a repetition of Locke's primary qualities.

Although Kant explained, first, that the nature of the objective world depends on our apperceptive ability, he later insisted that our apperceptive ability must correspond to the things created—in any case, their nature is such that they must remain a secret from us! Since relation, substance, and causality—in brief, all the properties that make up the identity of real things—are thought by the human mind, what remains of the thing itself behind our thought processes? Followed to their logical conclusion, Kant's methods lead eventually to subjectivism and spiritism. Berkeley had taken that road, and Fichte had followed him. But Kant remained standing fearfully in the middle of the road. At one moment he declared all things merely the result of our apperceptive ability; the next, trying to peer behind his own shadow picture, he gave this appearance a foundation in the absolute.

Wishing to fortify science with a theory of apodicticity and universality, Kant raised the problem of judgment. Starting with the proposition that there are analytic and synthetic judgments, and laying down the rule that, by their a priori nature, apodicticity and universality are the criteria for scientific truth, he put himself the question: How are synthetic a priori judgments possible? These judgments may not be derived from our knowledge, nor from our experience. This question of synthetic a priori judgments is the seed from which springs the whole *Critique of Pure Reason.*

But the fact is that there are no synthetic judgments, nor any a priori ones—much less synthetic a priori ones. Synthetic a priori judgments, Kant claimed, can be found in the rules of mathematics. $7 + 5 = 12$ is an a priori judgment; first, because the predicate is not contained in the subject; secondly, because it is not derived from experience. Both these statements, of course, are false. Seven plus five equals twelve is a simple analytical judgment of the experience of the identity of the total. Seven plus five contains no more nor less than twelve; it is only a question of the sum of twelve empirical units, even if the units have become abstracted. Numbers are no less empiric than words; they are both pictures of empirical factors and as such are derived from experience. There is no more a pure a priori mathematics than there is a pure a priori natural science derived from loose a priori ideas.

As an example of pure a priori science, Kant cites the law, "The sum total of matter cannot be either increased or decreased." Everyone will agree that in the concept "sum" the concept of "totality" is included, the impossibility of increase. The judgment that the sum of matter cannot be increased or decreased is a simple judgment of the identity of the total. Totality implies sum and sum, totality.

The next Kantian example is similar: "Every effect has a cause." Effect implies causation, and it means something that has been caused. Were this judgment synthetic, we should be able to think of effects which were *not* caused, and we would not need to seek the cause of everything that happens. But this is difficult to conceive. To happen means to be caused, and to be caused means to happen; a simple judgment of the identity of the total.

It is impossible to think otherwise. There is no judgment which predicates that which is not already in the subject. The predicate must be contained in the subject or the judgment is nonsensical. Such judgments as a squared circle, colorless paint, solid fluid—judgments in which the predicate is outside the sphere of the subject—would be synthetic judgments. In these cases, the predicate says more than is contained in the subject; in all other cases the predicate is, as it should be, analytic.

Kant's moral philosophy assumes, even more than his metaphysics, the appearance of scientific thoroughness. From the very beginning, however, Kant falls into the contradictions of Scholasticism. Virtue, he says, is possible only if God exists; therefore the truth of God's existence follows.[242] So in order to prove the reality of virtue, Kant grasps at the reality of God, and in order to find a basis for the postulate of the reality of God, he grasps at the reality of virtue—just as Baron Munchausen lifted himself by his own bootstraps.

According to Kant, we can reach the summit of virtue only in the other world. Morality, then, is the teaching of how to become worthy of celestial blessedness.[243] The idea that the individual will be rewarded for ethical conduct in the afterlife does not square with what Kant has said elsewhere, namely, that a deed done with the expectation of reward is not ethical. But Kant tried, as far as he could, to harmonize his philosophy with traditional Christian ethics. Naturally, therefore, God appeared to him as benevolent, just, wise, and so on.[244]

In his effort to establish a norm for morality, Kant postulated the Categorical Imperative. This Imperative bids us "act according to such law that we may desire that it should become universal." But the revolutionist, for instance, wants destruction; the anarchist, lawlessness; the conservative, traditionalism raised to the dignity of law; and each will conduct himself accordingly. In the last analysis, each man raises a different principle to universal law and, instead of the promised regulative absolute, achieves a completely subjective and superficial control.

In his introduction to *The Critique of Pure Reason*, Kant summed up his philosophy quite well when he stated as its aim: "I had to lift the sciences so as to make room for faith." After measuring up to his efforts to limit the sciences by investigating the possibility of knowing things in themselves, he discovered the distinction between positivism and spiritualism. He left the field of science for religion and postulated the freedom of the soul, its life after death, and the existence of a wise and all-creating God.

JOHANN GOTTLIEB FICHTE

Johann Gottlieb Fichte (1762-1814), who won great esteem for his elucidation of the Kantian "intelligible ego," evolved a metaphysics that is a mixture of Kant and Berkeley. Fichte expresses it in such phrases as: "I am because I am." "The ego posits itself." "I posit the ego in contrast to the non-ego." "I posit in the ego a partial ego in contrast to the partial non-ego." Let us explain, in an attempt to clarify these fundamental Fichtean axioms, that the ego and the non-ego separate from each other only gradually. The non-ego is but a mild form of the ego![245]

Just what is this ego? It is the other-worldliness in us,

115

it is "the absolutely real." There is, indeed, nothing besides the ego. All planets and solar systems are no more than positings of the ego.

We have already heard this nonsense from Berkeley, even to the idea that the world ceases to be once the ego stops producing it. Fichte disdained even to recognize those who might not believe in his ego-idealism, but made the mistake of accepting things as "real." But it is in the following quotation that we come to realize what passed for philosophy with him: "From the very beginning of the world to this day, religion, in whatever form it may have appeared, was metaphysics. Metaphysics is the essence of religion." [246] As might be expected, Fichte's later years found him plunged hopelessly into religion and mysticism.

The practical philosophy of Fichte is evocative of a certain amount of humor. Thus he said of the rights of women: "Woman is always subjected, in virginity to her father, in wedlock to her husband. On this ground it is out of the question for the state to give a woman a position unless with the express stipulation that she never marry for, if she does marry, the position becomes wedded to her husband along with all her other possessions." [247]

Further: "In normal women no sexual desires are noticeable, and in fact they really have none." "The woman may submit to her husband only to please him, because she makes herself the means to his end out of love." "The dignity of a woman lies in her complete subjection to her husband." [248]

Johann Fichte is the typical representative of German middle-class philosophy. His vigorous *Lectures on the German Nation* harp on the distinctions which were supposed to make the Germans a "chosen people." Fichte told the German Philistines that they were the oldest race, the bringers of salvation, and that by their spirit the world would be saved. For him the Germans were "The Nation." If Germany declined, the whole world would decline, without the least show of resistance.

This chauvinistic talk contributed not a little to perverting the German mind and imbuing its youth with a fanatical national pride and a hatred of foreigners. Fortunately, the more educated classes of Germany rejected this doctrine.

FRIEDRICH WILHELM SCHELLING

A follower of Fichte, Friedrich Wilhelm Schelling (1775-1854), was an eclectic who changed his view on life at least five times. He was forever involved in polemics, eager to argue his faith of the moment with fanatic zeal.

In his first period, he clung dogmatically to the "transcendent ego" of Fichte. "Everything is only in the ego and for the ego. In the ego philosophy found its *en kei pan* after bidding the highest price for victory." [249]

But Schelling's Fichteanism did not meet with the master's wholehearted approval. Controversies between them grew, and soon Schelling recognized the unreliability of Fichte's science. Next, he threw himself into the natural sciences, without however being able to adopt the empiric method. What he created in this, his second, period, is not physics but metaphysics. It has no solid scientific foundation. For instance, he wrote: "Sensibility is potential magnetism." "Weight is for itself the complete and invisible God." And: "Light is that which produces in inanimate nature the creative drive that functions in organic nature." [250]

These daring matters occupied our philosopher for only a few years. Then he fell under the spell of Spinoza.

With Spinozaism, Schelling ended his "merely reasonable, negative philosophy"; he threw himself now into the arms of a transcendental, positive philosophy. The products of this change of mind were certain postulates regarding revelation and mythology, as well as variations on Böhme and Neoplatonism. In this, his weakest, period, Schelling became known at the German courts as the man who could bring peace in the war between science and religion.

It is indeed on record that Schelling said, "Religion is

the pivot around which everything moves." Also on record are his preachments as to the soul's fall from grace and the necessity of its purification during the period of transmigration—gospels which go back to Neoplatonic days. Also recorded is the doctrine he inherited from the Görlitzian shoemaker, Böhme, concerning God and the Devil. Though the artistic turn of his mind caused the younger school of exact scientists to discredit his fanciful notions, and to deride him as the founder of "speculative physics," his philosophy of nature attracted considerable attention throughout Europe. Some of his main ideas have since won support in scientific circles.

GEORG WILHELM FRIEDRICH HEGEL

Not seduced by the apparent achievements of contemporary science, Georg Wilhelm Friedrich Hegel (1770-1831) undertook a restoration of the Aristotelian-Platonic gospel of transcendence. He restored the "Idea" to its place of honor as "a creative substance in constant motion." In a sense, the creative power of the Hegelian Idea is another definition of the Fichtean idealistic Ego. The understanding of reason is the inner essence of things—which is nothing more than Fichteanism in Platonic dress. That Hegel posited his Idea as existing in objective as well as subjective form, does not alter the fact that, along with Fichte and Berkeley, he belongs with those philosophers who want to break down reality. On the same principle, a fly might conceive the universe as no more than the imagination of a fly, which would disappear upon the fly's death.

The world as Idea—that is the end, as well as the beginning, of German idealism. Of course, the Idea, the spirit, does not stand alone. God is behind it. God is always behind the metaphysician. The spirit unfolds itself, realizes itself —that is, God acts, or in Hegel's terms, the history of the world is the justification of God in history. And all that has happened, or is now happening, is not only not without God, but is itself the work of God.[251]

Since God, or reason, undergoes development, there must be something to spur this development—that is, a hindrance or obstacle. This obstacle is the antithesis of reason in nature. Accordingly, to Hegel reason is a thesis and an antithesis at one and the same time. Analogous to Fichte's ego and non-ego, Hegel includes his antithesis in the Idea itself. In this sense, to Hegel philosophy meant the struggle of God with Himself and with nature.[252]

At the same time, Hegel did not forget to provide a crutch for the support of the trinal unity of God. He declared that humanity had been estranged from God, but that Jesus had re-established their former harmony. If Hegel's Christ teachings are not convincing, what he taught in another connection has the ring of absolute truth. He said: "Philosophy treats the same matters as religion, only in different form." [253]

It is obvious why the German conservative classes took reactionary philosophers like Fichte, Schelling and Hegel under their wing. No matter where their minds wandered, these philosophers remained loyal to the reactionary state governments, and while prisons and scaffolds were peopled with social reformers fighting for liberty, these philosophers proposed the simple panacea of resurrection in the next world and subjection in this one.

As a political philosopher, Hegel did not greatly deviate from the theories of his ruling class. "The land without a monarch," he observed, "is a formless chaos and is no longer worthy to be called a state." [254] The state expresses the will of God, but without a monarch it expresses nothing. Again: the sovereignty of the people (or the rabble, as Hegel preferred to call them) is one of the rabble's insane ideas. Things will never go as they should without a kingly ruler.

But the rabble has decided otherwise. It has not agreed that Hegel's state is "really ethical." States without monarchs have come into being in spite of the will of Hegel's God, because the people began to suspect that the "will of God" was almost invariably on the side of those who ruled.

Hegel also created a philosophy of nature. Here is a sample of it, offered without comment: "When the ether had emanated its absolute indifference into the indifference of light, to create a manifold plurality, and had given out its inner reason and totality in the far-flung system of the flowers of the solar system, the individuums of light are destroyed in the multiplicity, but those in which the circling leaves must stand out in stark individuality find universality of the form; the unity of these lacks the pure unity and neither has the absolute concept as such within itself. So also is the ethical system of the outspreading flower of the heavenly system kept together, and the absolute individuum is completely united in the universal and the real, or bodily in its highest form, together with the soul. For the multiplicity of the body is nothing else than the abstract idea, the absolute concept of pure individuation by which these things can become part of the absolute system." [255]

FRIEDRICH ERNST DANIEL SCHLEIERMACHER

Following in the footsteps of Fichte and Schelling, the preacher and theologian, Friedrich Ernst Daniel Schleiermacher (1768-1834), championed an aesthetic religious philosophy based on a "feeling of infinity." Theoretically, Schleiermacher went back to Spinoza and Plato. His preachments and meditations are obscured by a dank cloud of metaphysical sentimentality.

Schleiermacher's philosophy is based entirely on transcendentalism. There is not a single healthy idea in it.

JOHANN FRIEDRICH HERBART

Parallel with the scientific opposition to the so-called idealistic philosophers, near the beginning of the nineteenth century appeared a philosophic pseudo opposition which ended in an improved Kantianism.

Among the more earnest philosophers, Johann Friedrich Herbart (1776-1841) pleaded for a realistic philosophy which would offer guidance for the proper formulation of our concepts. Herbart discovered that our physical concepts—by which he meant our concepts of nature—contain contradictions. The clarification of these concepts, he decided, should be the business of philosophy. The absurdity of relying on metaphysical tools for the correction of scientific concepts is, of course, obvious. Only intensive scientific investigation can correct false concepts of nature.

In his logic, Herbart, who called himself a Kantian,[256] deviated little from his master, although he showed greater appreciation of psychological and pedagogical values. But Herbart was never able to free himself of his metaphysical ties. He saw in the purposiveness of natural phenomena of the omnipotence of God, the great artist, and declared this proof was as obvious as the existence of the soul. He called for faith in a "personal omnipotent God who is outside of and the creator of the world," and who must be served with humility and gratitude.

Another representative of the pseudo opposition to idealism, Arthur Schopenhauer, held a somewhat grimmer view of the purposiveness of the world and the nature of the Deity.

ARTHUR SCHOPENHAUER

The youth of Arthur Schopenhauer (1788-1860) was blighted by the marriage of his father to a gifted authoress nearly twenty years younger. After the elder Schopenhauer's suicide, his young widow Joanna had a number of affairs with other men. This incurred the bitter disapproval of her step-son, and led him to accuse her of his father's death. The conflict between them eventually terminated in a complete break.

Schopenhauer, to whom the world had shown its darkest side from the time he was a child, drew ever deeper into himself. Physical misfortune was added to early melancholy and the consequence was great sexual suffering. Spiritually and mentally aged before his time, Schopenhauer retreated into seclusion, his only companion a poodle he named Athman, "World-Soul." "I must confess," he once said, "that the sight of an animal makes me instantly happy and causes my heart to leap. . . . On the other hand, the sight of a man arouses in me the strongest feelings of disgust." [257]

For the tortured recluse there was no comfort in this world. The world, he whimpered, was ruled by vipers, while over everything reigned the scourges of syphilis and war. "It is far more accurate to say that the world was created by the Devil than that it was made by God." [258]

Schopenhauer passed his days in melancholy thought and mystic speculation, a constant prey to anxiety. "Even when I have nothing to worry about, I am worried lest there be something of which I am ignorant about which I ought to be worrying. *Misera conditio nostra.*" [259] The arrow of his bitterness was directed at everyone, but especially at women and Jews, whom he castigated with the most unflattering nicknames. Numerous are the stories which reveal his sickly hatred of mankind.

Schopenhauer's philosophy mirrors its author's temperament. It bristles with contradictions, infatuation with extremes, one-sidedness. In his chief work, *The World As Will and Idea,* Schopenhauer identifies nature with pure imagination. (*Cf.* Berkeley, Kant and Fichte.) He considers Kant's greatest achievement his distinction between the world in itself and the world as phenomenon. As to the "world in itself," Schopenhauer is more specific than Kant; he identifies it with the Will. This Will, he tells us, is the absolute in endless form. The world we see is merely the visible form of the Will.

122

This reminds us of Schelling's pronouncement: "The absolute is a will desiring to reveal itself in endless ways, forms and potentialities, and the world is the expression of this will."

This quotation reveals the unmistakable source of Schopenhauer's theory, though in his conclusions he deviates from Schelling. "The genital organs are in reality the burning foci of the Will." And again: "The desire for the act of copulation, that is the end and goal of all beings." [260]

About the world of the mind, Schopenhauer's thinking moves in a constant seesaw. At one time he declares that thought is merely a function of the brain, at another that the mind is only the creation of thought. It was the conflict between the natural scientist and the metaphysician in Schopenhauer which led him into these irresolvable contradictions.

In his hatred of sex, the area in which he had suffered so much, the victim preached: Negate the will to live! Happiness in this world, optimism about life, is a crime. True ethical conduct lies in the negation of the will to live. The end of everything is extinction, that Nirvana which the faithful experience at the feet of Buddha.

The leitmotif of Schopenhauer's philosophy is mystic meditation, since for man merciless nature has but one end, extinction.

With the death of Hegel, the creative period of these philosophic trends in Germany came to an end. Followers of particular systems continued to dispute among themselves, writing treatises and battling the old masters with a zeal worthy of a better cause. The works dedicated to such fruitless discord are endless; educated Germany was swamped with metaphysical literature. She also remained the country most burdened with metaphysics. Kantians, Fichteans, Hegelians, Herbartians, Spinozaists and Neoplatonists—all simmered and stewed as in a witch's cauldron.

JAKOB FRIEDRICH FRIES

Among the participants in these movements, only Jakob Friedrich Fries (1773-1843) makes some bid to originality by his discovery that it is impossible to arrive at Kantian transcendental philosophy save by way of psychology.

Hatred of the Jews permeates the thinking of Fries as well as other German idealistic philosophers. Fries demanded their extirpation "root and branch," or by "adopting the police regulations of Pharaoh and throwing their male children into the water." [261]

Fries and his fellows had little to offer in political science and social theory. We need merely note that at this time the philosophy of Thomas Aquinas was established by papal encyclical as the official Catholic science—which meant that the intellectual development of the youth in Catholic institutions of learning was to be arrested once and for all.

AUGUSTE COMTE

Auguste Comte (1798-1857) was the next man to initiate a new epoch in philosophy. Comte's private life was rich in adventure and eccentricity. In his youth he was acquainted with the noted old Socialist, Saint Simon, and was permanently influenced by his social theories. Comte's marriage with a former prostitute brought about his mental breakdown. In 1826, before he had written his major work, he suffered an attack of madness and had to be confined in an asylum. There his condition improved, but even after his release from the institution he suffered recurrences of the malady.

His friendship with Madame Clotilde de Vaux, the wife of a condemned criminal, proved one of the major influences in his life. After her early death, Comte's passion for her took an unmistakably morbid turn. During her life, he had organized a religious order of which he was the high priest.

124

He developed a catechism, a calendar of saints, holy days, sacraments and prayers of devotion. The object of adoration in this religion was the "Great Being" *(Grand Etre)*, Humanity. Prescribed prayers were offered up for two hours daily in the presence of a beloved person. Clotilde was Comte's symbol of a Positivist virgin, intercessor between humanity and its high priest.[262] As their altar the faithful used the chair on which Clotilde used to sit when she visited Comte.

As high priest of Humanity, Comte prescribed for himself a regular salary, which he augmented by applying to his friends for financial assistance. When three Englishmen showed reluctance to give the expected aid, he wrote in anger to John Stuart Mill, urging him "to spread the new philosophy in England among *abstract* adherents." On July 6, 1848, Comte broadcast an appeal to all people of the Western world to send money to him, the mainstay of Positivism.

In 1857 the founder of the philosophical school known as positivism breathed his last, having the previous year completed a philosophy of mathematics. Sects descending from his religious order are still to be found in Europe and in some parts of America.

Comte's great philosophical accomplishment was his claim for a special place for philosophy among the sciences. His so-called law of the three stages explains the passage of human thought through three periods of development: a theological stage, a second or transitional metaphysical stage, and a positive stage in which observation alone is the universal criterion of truth. Philosophy itself is the systematization of all scientific knowledge. But for Comte the unity of science is purely methodological, and he makes sociology, the science which he founded, the key to the understanding of political, psychological, and moral facts. Long after speculative philosophy had lost its prestige through separation from the other sciences, Comte announced, with complete seriousness, that the sciences should concern themselves only with facts. Thus he would have metaphysics, which had lost its own ground to the sciences, prescribe their duties, determine their limits, and combine their individual accomplishments. The flaws in his argument are obvious. It is absurd to ask the empiric investigator to submit to the guidance and control of the metaphysician. During all the years of the rise of positive knowledge, metaphysical speculation failed to shed light on real problems, or to enhance our thinking ability, or to improve the human condition in general. There is little reason to suppose that metaphysics will be more productive in the future.

As for the unification of the separate sciences, this goal is imbedded deep within the very principle of science. When removed from the empirical realm, it invites confusion of thought. Comte's work, though compendious, is uneven and no longer widely read. Still, his positive outlook has a place in the evolution of modern scientific philosophy.

HERBERT SPENCER

In essence a follower of Comte, Herbert Spencer (1820-1903) also devoted himself to finding an acceptable place for hard-pressed speculative philosophy. Having discovered that science deals with only partially unified knowledge, he suggested that philosophy take over the task of completely unifying knowledge. He declared that, though the sciences aim at completely unified knowledge, and summarize their findings in generalizations of an ever higher order, "philosophy is the truth of all general truths." In his *Principles* he says that the truths of philosophy stand in the same relation to the truths of science as the truths of both stand to truths of a lower category. But with this very statement Spencer renders philosophy unnecessary; for if the truths of philosophy differ from those of science only in degree and not in principle, then the task of science (striving for simplification and generalization) includes that of philosophy and makes the latter superfluous.

126

In spite of his strict Positivist philosophy, Spencer exhibits a certain religious mysticism. He indulges in such statements as: "The universal and positive truth is this: the power which reveals itself to us through the universe is unknowable." [263] This knowledge he attains via religion; he accepts the happy union of religion and science because both are based on the unknowable "world-ground." The Spencerian marriage of philosophy, as the highest science, with religion, which springs from the void of the unknowable, is but another unsuccessful attempt to accommodate superstition.

FRIEDRICH WILHELM NIETZSCHE

The philosophy of Friedrich Wilhelm Nietzsche (1844-1900) is a matter less for historical investigation than for psychological analysis. The product of Nietzsche's diseased mind is so vague in meaning that one of its greatest students could say: "It is undeniable that regarding the real essence of Nietzsche's philosophy there is still a great lack of clarity." [264]

In Nietzsche, philosophy achieved one of its most curious expressions, and it is ironic that the inflated, aristocratic theories of this nerve-disordered philologist should have become the shibboleths of the masses he belabored so vindictively. Perhaps slaves *do* fall in love with the morality of oppression, or perhaps the humblest of men sees himself in the superman who towers above the masses.

We have already suggested that modern psychiatry concerns itself too little with the morbid phenomena of metaphysics and religion. A probing analysis of these imaginary sciences would bring to light much significant material and contribute greatly to an understanding of present-day events. The dogmatism of our time is so great that a thorough medical and historical examination of the old authors, leaders and preachers of the transcendent is needed to dispel these persistent, many-colored superstitions. Unhappily, the study of the mind is still strongly influenced by metaphysical considerations. A forthright medical examination of the functions of the so-called soul and mind, excluding all metaphysics from the field, is in order.

Friedrich Nietzsche is one of the most interesting subjects for historical psychoanalysis. After the death of his father, who suffered from a mental disease, he remained under the care of his feminine relatives. With their coddling they developed in the boy a boundless pride, which later grew to abnormal proportions.

Even in his youth, Nietzsche felt himself called to a great task, whose nature he did not yet know. After a few unimportant essays and philological studies, he wrote to Strindberg: "I am the most independent and perhaps the strongest mind that exists today, condemned to a great task." And in the same year he wrote his sister: "I have *to speak plainly*, the future of all mankind is in my hands." And to his mother: "Seriously, your old sheep is now a very famous beast; not particularly in Germany, the Germans are too stupid and too mean to understand the loftiness of my mind." A shrewd Pole, playing upon Nietzsche's vanity, brought him documents purporting to prove that he was a descendant of the noble Polish family Nietzky. Nietzsche made quite a fuss about these ancestral "lords" and wrote: "Only thanks to his lineage has anyone a right to philosophize; here, too, ancestry and blood are decisive."

Nietzsche's passion for originality and the bizarre was unquenchable. Everything social was repugnant to him. "That which can become social has little value. Where the people eat and drink, even where they pray, there it stinks." "Graf Nietzky" wanted philosophers to be different: "True philosophers are imperative; they say, thus should it be!" Above all, the philosopher must keep aloof from the herd. "And have your mask and ornament ready that you may be esteemed, even feared a little!"

That is it—be feared! That is a sure way of getting attention. Nietzsche admired everything that inspired fear. He spoke reverentially of the bestial Caesar Borgia as "the personification of the greatest health." As for women, Nietzsche had his own way of handling them. "Do you go to women? Don't forget the whip!" And for man and wife he had this advice: "Thus do I wish man and wife to be; the one, warring; the other, fertile; both dancing with *head and foot!*" [265]

This philosopher yearned for something greater, stronger, more awe-inspiring than anything that had yet been—the superman who "plays horseshoes with the gods at their earthly feast so that the earth trembles, splits open, and emits a stream of fire." [265]

Nietzsche's alleged "love letters" to his sister Elizabeth were deliberate falsifications from the pen of that mercenary woman.

Nietzsche was in love with big words. He felt that he truly inspired fear with such expressions as: "Destroy, destroy unto me the good and the just." He spurned the just. He wanted to be evil, very evil, fearfully evil.

"Raise your hearts, oh brethren, higher, higher. Forget not your feet. Raise your feet, you splendid dancers. Better yet, *stand on your heads!*"

Nietzsche's call for dancing and laughter, as well as his belief in his mission as a redeemer, made fatal inroads on his role as a hard-boiled inspirer of awe. In the last weeks before his breakdown, he played with the idea of appearing as the one and only true disciple of Christ.[266]

Nietzsche adored the paradoxical, the spectacular, the playful, the absurd and the dazzling. He was the most honor-thirsty of German authors. He prescribed masks for philosophers, and donned one himself—but behind the mask lurked pride and insanity.

Nietzsche had suffered from headaches since early childhood. His pain grew worse each year. In 1889 he suffered an attack which was followed by paralysis of the brain, and for ten years he lived in utter darkness, until another attack mercifully put an end to his life.

HENRI BERGSON

Henri Bergson (1859-1941), who argued the superiority of the "inner emotions" over natural reason, reached back into ancient metaphysics. To grasp the truth of inner being, Bergson warned, we must break with our scientific habits of thought. The business of the intellect is only with the dead matter that surrounds us, but life itself is accessible to the intuition.

Any metaphysician or theologian will agree, Bergson declared, that only those things can be called true which have been grasped intuitively, without having been subjected to an intermediate process of meditation, abstraction or generalization. The true task of philosophy is to reveal that world which remains forever closed to the intellect.[267]

In order to reach into "life," the mind must overpower itself. By means of an unreflective mode of thought, the mind can grasp "fluid concepts" and pursue reality through all its twistings and turnings, and thus "grasp the motion of the inner life." [268] Bergson's theories of *"élan vital," "la durée," "la conscience,"* and so on, reveal his close relation to the Platonic and Schelling dream systems.

But how the intellect, robbed of every higher function, can invigorate instinct so that, *"élargé et épuré,"* it can, as intuition, re-establish the unity of the stream of life, remains Bergson's secret.[269] We cannot hope for an adequate explanation of "intuition" since, in his view, only the intellect possesses language, whereas intuition lies too deep in the inner world to be reached by words. Of this much we can be certain: this philosophy leads to the idea of "a free and independent God." [270]

And with this notion we are right back where we started, at the time of Parmenides, when that mystic teacher, having completed his discourse on the inner world, begged the reader's forgiveness for leading him next to natural science—the study of the outer world—since there the intuitive certainty which guided the understanding of inner reality, no longer functioned. Bergson thus shares one experience with virtually all his predecessors: he sees most clearly when the light of natural reason is extinguished.

WILLIAM JAMES

Of the modern philosophies of value, that which has found the largest audience in Anglo-Saxon countries is Pragmatism. This very American philosophy—the judgment of the reality of things according to their usefulness and practical applicability—was first advanced as a philosophy of value by Charles Peirce in 1878.[271] Thirty years later several English and American philosophers took it up, among whom the most prominent was William James (1842-1910).

James declared that there is no truth in ideas as such. Truth enters only when the idea proves itself practical and of use.[272] Examined more closely, this notion proves to be an old friend with a new name. What James does is simply redefine the hypothesis of universality. All sciences make use of this principle, that a hypothesis is valid as long as it operates or is useful.

The difference between the hypothesis of the sciences and the Pragmatic theory of truth is this: The scientist, in spite of his factual tendencies, accepts the hypothesis as just that, without ascribing to it any absolute reality. Moreover, he is quite ready to abandon it once a better explanation is found for facts the hypothesis has only partially explained. The Pragmatist, however, accepts the idea as true absolutely once it has proved its practical value.

"The true idea is determined by its practicability," says James. This notion, which is logically untenable, leads in practice to some rather odd consequences. The claim which an idea lays to practical value (at one time James calls it "cash value") depends upon thousands of shifting circumstances and personal preferences. Ideas which work satisfactorily in J⌃mes's eyes might seem quite evil in the eyes of someone else. And vice versa.

131

James said, for instance, "According to the Pragmatic principle, the hypothesis of God is true in the widest sense of the word if it works satisfactorily." But where can one find a definition of "a satisfactorily working idea" that is even remotely satisfactory? [273] Are not different individuals satisfied by different, often opposing, ideas?

As long as Pragmatism makes the value of an idea depend on its practicalness, it follows, superficially, the principle of the scientific hypothesis. But when James makes this hypothesis a criterion of truth and reality, he falls into the pseudo rationalism of that metaphysics which can so easily convert the unreal into the "real" and the real into the "unreal."

Besides, for what reason should we identify the truth of an idea with its practical value? Is it not more logical to say: "This idea is applicable, useful, workable, and the like"—rather than to philosophize: "This idea is *true* because it is applicable, useful, workable, and the like." The attribute of truth is, in this case, superfluous, even misleading. The concept of usefulness, drawn from experience itself, is sufficient for the purposes for which the judgment is made. All other philosophic attributes hide meaning rather than contribute to its clarification.

James called himself "a hard man," and he fought the weak metaphysicians with courage. It is to his enduring credit that he battled earnestly for the motto: "Look away from primary substances, principles, categories, apodictic necessities, and look to the end of things, the fruits, the consequences, and the actualities."

JOHN DEWEY

The unique influence of John Dewey (1859-1952) on American education is rooted in his philosophy of instrumentalism, first expressed in his *Studies in Logical Theory* (1903) where he acknowledged his indebtedness to William James. Born on a farm in Vermont, he credited his early surroundings with focusing his attention on the importance of individual freedom and fortifying his faith in the essential union of the democratic and philosophical spirit. At the celebration of his ninetieth birthday, he declared that losing faith in our fellow men means losing faith in ourselves, "and that is the unforgivable sin."

Recognized by common consent as America's leading philosopher, he made inquiry, rather than truth or knowledge, the essence of logic. It was from the great philosophical streams of nineteenth-century Europe that he drew his initial inspiration. From Hegel and Marx he received the incentive to explore the complexity of the institutions in which human beings are enmeshed; from Darwin the evolutionary view that thought is an outgrowth of an organism's struggle to adapt to its environment together with the notion that thinking may be interpreted in terms of the resolution of conflict and tension; and from the great educators of Europe the conviction that an effective system of public education is the mainspring of a democratic society.

Dewey's own distinctive views began to take shape as he turned against German philosophy, under the influence of William James, and repudiated the separation of the individual and the social. "Experience" and "learning by doing" became the watchwords of his new theory of instrumentalism, which he defined as "an attempt to constitute a precise logical theory of concepts, judgments and inferences in their various forms, by primarily considering how thought functions in the experimental determinations of future consequences." He examines the way in which ideas, taken as solutions of specific problems, function within a wider context. His criterion of truth lies within, rather than beyond, a situation of life that can be shared. In his democratic philosophy, common life is the reality of a dignity equivalent to that of nature or the individual.

The failure of human intelligence in social areas prompted Dewey to stress the social and pedagogical aspects of his philosophy of instrumentalism. Aware of the crucial role of education in the survival of democratic institutions, for more than forty years he maintained a position of leadership in education, bringing increased human interest into school life and work, enlarging the role of pupil initiative and responsibility. Many of his writings on education typify the reformist fervor of his time and constitute the theoretical framework of the Progressive movement.

GEORGE SANTAYANA

Though he spent many of his productive years in Europe, George Santayana (1853-1952) has a place, with Dewey and James, in the pantheon of American philosophers. The son of a Spanish father and an American mother, he hints at his own Spanish strain when he describes the southern mind as long-indoctrinated, disillusioned, distinct, skeptical, malicious, yet in its reflective phase detached and contemplative, able to despise all entanglements, to dominate will and to look truth in the eye without blinking. His original views, lucid intelligence, and mordant wit endeared him to a generation of students, whose companionship he preferred to that of his colleagues.

Although Santayana rejected organized religion, in his later works he stressed the role of faith in the life of man. One of the most striking features of his philosophy is his unrelenting materialism. He was "attached to Catholicism" but "entirely divorced from faith," and protested that his skepticism had rather confirmed than dispelled his attachment. He continued to hold that "most conventional ideals, the religious ones included, are not adequate to the actual nature and capacities of the men who accept them."

According to Santayana, the seat and principle of genesis is matter, not essence. Matter is in flux; mind is existentially carried along the movement of that flux. Knowledge is a compound of intuitive conviction and expectation, animal faith and intuition of essence. By means of essence, the pursuit, attention and feelings which contribute to knowledge are transcribed in aesthetic, moral or verbal terms into consciousness.

Santayana's *The Sense of Beauty* (1896) is perhaps the most important American work in the field of aesthetics. Concerned with "the nature and elements of our aesthetic judgments," it combines ideal or formal elements with an appreciation of its material aspect.

In his later works Santayana combined the wisdom of the old world and the new in works characterized by stylistic elegance as well as broad philosophical vision. Although convinced of the truth of his work, he did not except his philosophy from his general judgment of philosophical systems, which he regarded as personal, temperamental, even premature. All systems are human heresies, and the orthodoxy around which they play is no private or closed body of doctrine. It is "the current imagination and good sense of mankind," a body of beliefs and evaluations far too chaotic, subject to errors, and conventional to satisfy a reflective mind. Hence the need for personal philosophical inquiry and the impossibility of shaping a philosophy to satisfy all mankind.

BERTRAND RUSSELL

An eloquent champion of individual liberty in the social realm as well as in philosophy is Bertrand Russell (born in 1872) whose contribution to logic rivals that of Santayana to aesthetics. Admired by Albert Einstein, who stated that he owed "innumerable happiness to the reading of Russell's works," the British peer has been called the greatest logician since Aristotle.

The most controversial Anglo-Saxon philosopher of our century, Lord Russell has for years been persecuted because of his radical pacifism and unorthodox views on social and political issues. His appointment as professor of philosophy at the College of the City of New York in 1940 roused the fury of bigots of all denominations. It was denounced as "the establishment of a chair of indecency" after a trial had ended with his condemnation as "immoral" and a danger to the youth of the city. In recent months he has continued to stir the fires of controversy on the international scene, criticizing the mistreatment of Jews in Russia as well as American involvement in Vietnam. A prolific writer, he attributes the clarity and fluency of his style to the fact that he was not subjected to the influence of public school education.

Principia Mathematica (1910-13), written in collaboration with ALFRED NORTH WHITEHEAD, (1861-1947), provides the theoretical foundation of modern mathematical logic. Russell at first regarded mathematics as the ideal of philosophy, then as the instrument of science; finally he made logic the basis of a general theory of science.

Philosophy is regarded as something intermediate between theology and science. Like theology it is concerned with speculation, but like science it appeals to human reason rather than to authority. To achieve results useful to humanity, philosophy should take its problems from natural sciences rather than from theology or ethics. Knowledge is a subclass of true belief, but not every true belief is to be recognized as knowledge. Knowledge is an intimate, almost mystical contact between subject and object by perception, which is far more complicated than is generally supposed. Russell holds that all human knowledge is uncertain, inexact and partial, but that in its broad outline scientific knowledge is to be accepted.

In *Human Knowledge* (1948) Russell takes up the problem of the relation between individual experience and the general body of scientific knowledge. He maintains that science cannot be wholly interpreted in terms of experience, and the description of the world must be kept free from influences derived from the nature of human knowledge. Like Whitehead, he holds that the distinction between mind and body is a dubious one. It is better to speak of an organism, leaving the division of its activities between the mind and the body unspecified. Russell concludes that "cosmically and causally, knowledge is an unimportant feature of the universe."

LOGICAL POSITIVISM

Strongly influenced by Bertrand Russell and LUDWIG WITTGENSTEIN (1889-1951) was the leader of the group of neopositivists who met regularly in Vienna to discuss problems of common interest. Led by MORITZ SCHLICK (1882-1936), the group included philosophers such as RUDOLPH CARNAP and OTTO NEURATH (1882-1945) as well as mathematicians and scientists. The group was characterized by its hostility to metaphysics, its advocacy of modern symbolic logic, and its conviction that the true achievements of science can neither be destroyed nor altered by philosophy.

The tragic death of Schlick at the hands of a demented student put an end to a life devoted to the inquiry into the meaning of life. Schlick's aim was not to build a system but to investigate the way of philosophizing that satisfies the demands of the most scrupulous scientific conscience. He made a sharp distinction between experience which is immediate and knowledge which is not vision but rather calculation and organization by means of concepts and symbols. His radical empiricism leans upon Berkeley and Hume but profits from symbolic logic. The task of science is to obtain knowledge of reality; the task of philosophy is to interpret these achievements correctly and to expound their deepest meaning.

EXISTENTIALISM

The deepest meaning of human existence is the unifying theme of a diverse group of thinkers popularly called existentialists. The problem of man—his concrete existence, his contingency, his freedom, and his ultimate responsibility

for his actions—is central in the writings of KARL JAS-
PERS, MARTIN HEIDEGGER, and JEAN-PAUL
SARTRE. Chief among their philosophic forebears are
SOREN KIERKEGAARD (1813-1855), the Danish counterpart of Schopenhauer, and EDMUND HUSSERL (1859-
1938), the German thinker who gave new direction to
phenomenology, and Nietzsche, whose "God is dead" pronouncement fits into the context of atheistic humanism.

Karl Jaspers, born in 1883, has been the most respected
philosopher in Germany since the end of World War II. He
began his career as a psychiatrist—his *General Psycho-
pathology* (1913) offered a new classification of mental ill-
nesses—and focused his attention on the relations between
a philosopher's personality and his doctrine. It was from
the viewpoint of a psychiatrist that he first studied the
writings of Kierkegaard and Nietzsche. The true value of
man, according to Jaspers, lies not in the species or type
but in the situation of the individual or the conditions of
his existence. With him freedom, man's unique attribute, is
beyond objective knowledge and points to the rediscovery
of God from within.

Despite his leanings toward the socio-political views of
the Third Reich, Martin Heidegger (born in 1889) has a
considerable French following. He was strongly influenced
by Husserl and although he denies that he himself is an
existentialist, has had a decisive influence on the development of atheistic existentialism in France. The fine distinctions which he draws in analyzing being lead him to the
very core of personality, in which he discovers guilt, anxiety
and dread. In his main work *Sein und Zeit* (1927) he ex-
plores the question of man's utter loneliness and total isola-
tion. Only against the background of historical fate does
man's present existence attain value. [Yet Heidegger was
an ardent and persistent follower of Nazism.]

Though he is the point of confluence of three post-Heg-
elian streams of thought—the Marxist, the existentialist,
and the phenomenological—Jean-Paul Sartre (born in
1905) is profoundly and self-consciously individualistic in

his interpretation of the human situation. His major writings now span almost three decades and provide insights into the evolution of his thought from the resolution of the existential crisis through art (*Nausea*, 1938) to the discovery of personal meaning and values through the social function (*Search for a Method*, 1957; *Problems of Marxism*, 1964). The first major exposition of his doctrine of freedom is in the monumental but difficult *Being and Nothingness* (1943), which established his reputation as the leader of the philosophic movement generally associated with his name today. His analysis of the existential situation brilliantly illustrates the three classic stages which any theory, according to William James, must pass through: first it is "attacked as absurd; then it is admitted to be true but obvious and significant; finally it is seen to be so important that its adversaries claim that they themselves discovered it."

Educated in Paris, Sartre majored in philosophy and was strongly influenced by the writings of Heidegger, Kierkegaard, and Husserl, under whom he later studied at the University of Göttingen. He taught philosophy for several years but finally decided to devote all his time to writing. He now devotes much of his energies to editing the influential journal *Les Temps Modernes*, which he founded in 1946 in his search for a way to vindicate freedom and the value of the individual.

Sartre's refusal to accept the Nobel Prize for Literature is wholly consonant with the ideas expressed in his dramas, novels, and philosophical writings. The Sartrean concept of anguish subsumes man's intense awareness of his contingency and freedom: man enters an absurd world, makes it habitable through his consciousness, confers meaning on it through his free choice, and is overawed by the dreadful freedom which makes him solely responsible for his situation and his life. Anguish generated by man's recognition of his existential plight, man's inhumanity to man, man's search for social justice—these are the pervasive themes of Sartre's works.

NOTES

1. *Metaphysics*, I, 3; *De Coele*, II, 13; *De Anima*, I, 5.
2. Theophrastus, *Phys.*, 27, 17 and 154, 15; Aristotle, *Phys.*, 1, 4, p. 187 a and III, 4, p. 203.
3. Plac., III, 16.
4. Plut. Plac., I, 3.
5. Aristotle, *De Anima*, I, 2, p. 405 a, 21.
7. Simpl., *Phys.*, 159, 13.
8. Simpl. and *De Coele*, 586, 29; Ael. Nat. anim., 16, 29.
9. Galen, *Ad Hippocrates*, Ep. 6, 48.
10. Ael. Nat. Anim., 12, 7.
11. Simpl., 155, 23.
13. Diog., 10, 13.
14. Sambl. in Nic., p. 77, 9.
15. Stob. Ecl.
16. Lydus, *De Mens*, II, 12.
17. Aristotle, *Metaphysics*, 14, 3, p. 1091 a, 15, and *Physics*, 213 b, 22.
18. Eudemus Simpl., *Phys.* 732, 30D.
19. Aristotle, *De Anima*, I, 2, p. 404.
20. *Scholien zu Arist. Rhetoriki*, 13 p., i 373 b.
21. Plato, *Protagoras*, 337 D.
22. Aristotle, *Politics*, I, 3.
23. *Ibid.*, II a, 7.
24. Plato, *Apology*, 21 and 22.
25. Aristotle, *Metaphysics*, Xi, 4, 1078 b, 1731.
26. Diog., II, 94; Cicero, *Tuscan*, I, 83.
27. Diog., II, 108, and VII, 187.
28. Plato, *Republic*, 427 D.
29. *Ibid.*, 373.
30. Plato, *Nomoi*, 732 D; *Republic*, 437 D.
31. Plato, *Phil. Cap.*, 12-16.
32. *Phaedrus, Republic.*
33. Aristotle, *De Anima*, I, 4, p. 408 b., 32; Stob. Ecl., I, 62.
34. *The Birth and Development of Animals*, Iv, c 32.
35. *Ibid.*, IV, c. 32.

36. Aristotle, *Laws*, 10, 900 c.
37. Aristotle, *Politics*, I, 2.
38. *Ibid.*, I, 2 c, 14.
39. *Ibid.*, I, 2 c., 4 and 6.
40. *Ibid.*, I, 5 c, 9.
41. Aristotle, *Ethics*, III, 7, p. 113, b 6.
42. Aristotle, *De Anima*, 429 a, 15, and 430 a, 3.
43. Aristotle, *Poetics*, 9, p. 1451 b, 5.
44. Sext. M, 169.
45. Ep. 89, 4.
46. Diogenes Laertius, VII, 25.
47. Diogenes Laertius, VII.
48. Diogenes Laertius, VII, 87.
49. *Handbook of Morals*, III.
50. *Cf.* Spinoza, *De Deo*,
51. *Meditations*, II, 3.
52. *De Benef.*, VII, 23; *De Prov.*, 5.
53. Nat., II, 32.
54. *Meditations*, I, 6.
55. *Handbook of Morals*, II, 16, 17.
56. Nat., II, 37.
57. *Cf.*, Spinoza, *Ethics*, V.
58. Ep. 65, 16; 102, 22, Nat. Prol., 12.
59. Ep. I, 4, 16.
60. Athen., VII, p. 280 a.
61. Plac. Iv, 3; Lucretius, III, 18; II, 646; V, 146.
62. *De Benef.*, IV, 19.
63. *Op. Mund.*, 54.
64. *De Vita Mosis*, II, 140 M.
65. *De Decal.*, 18.
66. *Gen.*, 27, 40. *Quod omnis probus liber*, p. 454 M.
67. *Op. Mund.*, 140, 169.
68. *Div. haer.*, 92, *Plant.* 17, *Grundlegung zur Met d. Sitten.*
69. II B, *Moses*, 33, 23; *Erud.*, Gr. 108, *Fuga inv.*, 63, Decal., 73, 81.
70. John VIII, 48 ff.

71. Acts II, 22-36.
72. Gal., II, 20.
73. Acts XIV, 13.
74. Cor., 63, C, 10, XI, 10, VIII, 36.
75. Acts, XI, 1.
76. Gal. I, 1; Acts XV.
77. Acts XIII, 46.
78. Eusebius Pamphilius, *Vita Constantini*, lib. 4 cap. 27; Migne, *Patrologia Latina*, tom. 8, col. 77a.
79. S. Kol., I, 15; John 21:17; 4, 34; 20, 19, 26; 1:3; 10:13.
80. Revelation 29:3, 9; Matthew 21:321.
81. Tanchuma for I.B.M., 18, 17; II b.m., 34, 27; numeri r.k., 14; Tanchuma Buber, II, 116; Yalkut, 405; Exod. Rabba I 47; Tanchuma, I, p. 22 a: Chagia, 27 a; Numerui Rabba, K3.
82. Epiphanius, *Haer.*, 26, 10; 40, 5.
83. *Contra Haer.*, 1, 13.
84. Commentary on Matthew's 4th Homily, c. 3f.
85. *Cf.* Ambrosius, *On the Virgin;* Cyprian, *On the Conduct of Virgins.*
86. *On the Creation of Man*, c. 37.
87. V. 30.
88. Irenaeus, IV, 30.
89. *On the Greeks*, c. 47.
90. *Contra Arrian*, 2nd speech, c. 63.
91. *On the Creation of Man*, c. 9.
92. Mysteria, *cf.* Epiphanes, *Adv. Haer.*, LXVII, 14; August. C. Faust 21, 14.
93. Augustinus Contra Ep., Manich, c. 18; C. Faust 21.
94. Apiphanius, *Haeres* LXVI, 9.
95. S. Cotelerius, SSPP Apostaloricum op. Bd. I, S. 543; *Fihrist des Abulfaradsh Muhammed ben Ishak al Warrak*, edition G. Flugel, S. 9.
96. Augustinus, *De Morib.*, Manich, X, 19, 1.
97. *De Civitate Dei*, 19, 22; 13, 18; 14; 10; 11, 7; 12, 6.
98. *De Ord.*, I, 1007, and L, 993.
99. *Cf.* Conf. 7, 25; *De be. vit.*, 975; *De Gen., III*, 190.

142

100. *De Civitate Dei*, 19, 25.
101. Ep. 141, 5.
102. *De Civitate Dei*, 22, 8; 14, 25; Kant, *Critique of Practical Reason*.
103. *De nupt. et conc.*, I, 3.
104. *Correspondence of Pope Innocent and Hilarius*, 177-178.
105. *Cf.* Serm. 61, 23; 82, 4, 7.
106. *De Civitate Dei*, 11, 12; 12, 12; 11, 3.
107. Photius, cod. 251, p. 461 a, 24.
108. Porphyry, *Vita Plotini*, c. 17.
109. Enn., IV, 8.
110. *Ibid.*, I, 2 i.
111. Rep. X, 13.
112. Enn., I, 6; II, 9.
113. Pante arretos arche.
114. *Hier.*, VII, 3.
115. *Ibid.*, IV, 2.
116. *Concerning the Holy Name of God*, VII, 3.
117. *De Div.*, II, 15; *Ibid.*, I, 3c 17.
118. *De Praed.*, I, 1.
119. *Expos. in Coel. Hierarch.*, p. 205.
120. *De div.*, IV, 7; i, 4, 8; L. C., IV, 8.
121. Hiomr., *De Praedest. dissert. post*, c. 2, 5, 34.
122. Tertullian, Augustine.
123. *Philosophia ancilla theologiae*, edition Cajetan, i 743, III, S. 321.
124. *Monol. Praef.*
125. *De Fide Trin.*, C., I and II.
126. *Cur Deus Homo*, I; *Proslogium*.
127. *Proslogium*, II and III.
128. *Proslogium, V, IX; Monol.*, XLVII, C. D. C., II, 21. Even Spinoza repeats Anselm's thesis of God's love for himself. The acceptance of Scholastic concepts is one of the greatest weaknesses of Spinoza. See *Ethics*, V.
129. *Cur Deus Homo*, I, 1.
130. Buchari, III, p. 30; Ibn Hischam, I, p. 268.

131. Buchari, Al Sahih I, Koran, Sura, 96, 74, 65, 40, 8, 113.
132. Koran, Sura 13.
133. *Ibid.*, Sura 52.
134. *Ibid.*, Sura 61.
135. Ibn Hischam, p. 553.
136. Koran, Suras 2, 30, 49.
137. *Ibid.*, Suras 33, 49.
138. *Ibid.*
139. *Ibid.*
140. *Book of Ringstones*, c. 54.
141. *Ibid.*, c. 50 and 40 b, "Elements of Conduct."
142. "Introduction," I.
143. *Cf.* Ibn Khalikan, 189.
144. Cod, Rehm 81 f, 71 b.
145. Judah ha-Levi, Cusari, *The Opinion of Philosophers Concerning the Soul.* See also Sharistani.
146. *Elixir of Happiness.*
147. *Elements of Conduct*, I.
148. *Ibid.*
149. *Renaissance of Religion*, Book 12, Chapter X.
150. *Metaphysics*, Introduction.
151. *Ibid.*, IV.
152. *Philosophy and Theology*, II.
153. Schmolder, *Essai sur les écoles philosophies chez les Arabes*, p. 132.
154. *The Teachings of Faith*, III, 4; VI, 6; VII, 2; III, 4; IV, 1; VI, 2; VI, 6.
155. *Ibid.*, I, 2.
156. *Ibid.*, IX, 1; Kant, Critique of Practical Reason.
157. *Duties of the Heart*, VIII, 235b.
158. *Ibid.*, 25a.
159. Munk, *Literaturblatt d. Orients*, No. 46, 1846.
160. *Quelle*, IV, 1, 12.
161. *Zohar*, I, 16.
162. *Cf.* Maimonides' remark on the subject in a letter to Samuel Ibn-Tibbon; Also Aristotle, *Physics*, VIII, 2, p. 252 b 24-25.

163. Spinoza's relation to earlier Jewish philosophers is still not clear.
164. *Of the Great Faith*, pp. 70, 56, 63, 79, 45, 99, 128, 78, 98, 92.
165. Graetz, *History of the Jews*, VI, p. 316; Carmaly, *Annals*, p. 325; Munk, *Notices sur Josef ben Jehudah*, Archives Israelites, p. 319.
166. Fuehrer, I, 49, and II, 6.
167. Commentary on the Mischna and Mischna-Torah.
168. *Laws of Repentance*, III.
169. Fuehrer, I, 34, II, 23, III, 28, I, 58.
170. Kusari, I, 103, 63, 65; III, 53; V, 16.
171. *Comm. in Math.*, p. V.
172. *Theol.*, I, 19, 5-3.
173. *De Hom.*, 54 a, 5 p. 263c.
174. *De Trin.*, 2, art. 3.
175. *Contra Gent.* I c 9.
176. *Sent. Lib.*, III dist. 241 art. c.
177. *Theol.*, I, 32a.
178. *De Regimine Principium*, I.
179. *Theol.*, I, 92, 4; Aristotle, *De Anima*, I, II, c 3.
180. Compare *Encyclica Aeterni Patris des Papstes Leo*, Aug. 4, 1879.
181. *"Ergo autem ad positionem Avicembronis redeo. Voluntas est superior intellectu,"* Rep. Paris, vol. 42, no. 4.
182. *Op. Oxon. Prol.*, 4, 4; Rep. Paris. Prol. 3.
183. *"Philosophia infidelium est penitus nociva."* Opus Maius, II, c. 8.
184. *"Philosophia habet dare probationes fidei Christianae." Ibid.*
185. *"Soli enim patriarchae et prophetae fuerunt veri philosophi qui omnia sciverunt."* Philo. c. Theol. aff. c IX.
186. *Cf.* ad. I. Sen. 2 1 de sacr. alt. C 36.
187. *"Entia non sunt multiplicanda praeter necessitatem."* Tract. log. I.
188. *Docta Ignorantia*, II, 2.
189. *Ibid.*, II, 11; Cf. *De Coniecturis*.

145

190. Preiffer edition, p. 109.
191. *Ibid.*, p. 163, 136.
192. *Aurora*, 22, 12, 13.
193. *The Trinity of Life*, 4, 90; 5, 18.
194. *Ibid.*, 5, 13.
195. *Myst.*, 15, 24.
196. *Creation of Man*, II, 6, 7; *Forty Questions*, 28, 3; *Aurora*, 10, 61.
197. The German *"Quellgeist"* he derives from the Latin *"Qualitas"*!
198. *Aurora*, 21, 23, 55; 21, 19, 26, 101; 22, 90; 24, 14, 26, 20; 21, 4; and *On Three Principles*, 14, 4.
199. Dr. Abraham Hinckelmann.
200. *De Monade*, 80; *De Minimo*, 74; *Oratio Valedictoria*, c. 10; *De Immenso*, 500; *Della Causa*, 11.
201. *Della Causa*, II.
202. Lagarde edition, 721, 16; 713, 3.
203. *Eroica Furori;* Lagarde, 707, 17.
204. *Collection of the Proceedings in the House of Commons Against the Lord Verulam, Viscount St. Albans, Lord Chancellor of England for Corruption and Bribery,* London, 1722, p. 25.
205. Epist. I, 2, 24. 25.
206. *Ibid.*, II, 53.
207. Letter of November 25, 1630.
208. Baillet, LII, 1, p. 38.
209. *Principles*, I, 27, Med. III, 20.
210. Med. V.
211. *Principles*, I, 28, 76; Epist. III, 250.
212. Med. V, 25-304.
213. *Principles*, I, c. 23.
214. *"Nihil est in nostris ideis, quod menti sive cogitandi facultati non feurit innatum (praeter causam occasionalem)."* Med. III.
215. *Cf.* Plato, *Phaedo,* 75b, and compare also the Stoics, who are called by Cicero, *"notiones communes sive innatae."*
216. Reg. III, 6.

217. *De passionibus*, I, 28 and 41; I, 16; II, ep. II, 26.
218. Willisium, *De Anima Brutorum*, c. I, 6.
219. *Princ. Phil.*, I c 5.
220. Sefer Hayashar, Sefer Harazim, Sefer Shem ben Noah, etc.
221. *Principles of Philosophy*, III; *Of the Citizen*, c. 11.
222. *Of the Citizen*, c. 6.
223. *Elements of Law*, p. 176.
224. Letter of dedication to Lord Devonshire, v. 1, N v. 1646.
225. *Seven Philosophical Problems with an Apology for Himself and His Writings.*
226. Entr. XIV, 13.
227. Rech. III, 1/2; III, 2/8.
228. *Traité de la nature*, S. Labrune, p. 39; Ent. VIII.
229. *Réflexions sur la promotion physique*, VIII, 23.
230. "*Nous voyons toutes choses en Dieux,*" Rech. 2, 6.
231. Entr. VI, 12.
232. *Works*, Gerhardt edition, II, 311; IV, 246.
233. *Monadologie*, 3, 9, etc.
234. IV, 514.
235. *Monadologie*, 4.
236. *Ibid.*, 81.
237. Works, III, 143; VII, 412.
238. Theodice c, 233.
239. "*In recidenda atomorum ratione confugiemus ad Deum denique.*"
240. *Cf.* Plato, *Theatet*, 176 a; *Laws*, X, 900 c; Plotinus Enn., II, 9.
241. *Critique of Pure Reason*, Introduction to second edition.
242. *Critique of Practical Reason*, II, V.
243. *Ibid.*, V, II, IV; II, V.
244. *Ibid.*, V, I, I, c. 8, Anm. 2; II, V.
245. *Wissenschaftlehre*, I, I, and II, 4.
246. *Die Grundzuege des Gegenwaertigen Zeitalters*, p. 533.
247. I, I, 3.

248. I, I, 4; I, I, 3; I, I, 33.
249. W. I, 193.
250. W. I, 439, II, 207, Schroeter edition.
251. *Philosophie der Deschichte.*
252. *Religionsphilosophie*, II, p. 286.
253. *Ibid.*, II, 287.
254. Vol. 7, II, p. 360, L. Michelet edition.
255. *"Ueber die Wissenschaftlichen Behandlungsarten des Naturrechtes," Krit. Journal des Philosophie*, Vol. II, 2 and 3, 1802-3.
256. *Vorrede zur Metaph.*, Vol. 1.
257. N.P., 363.
258. N.P., 316.
259. N.P., 658.
260. *Works*, Vol. I, p. 427.
261. *Ueber die Gefaehrdung des Wohlstandes und Charakters der Deutschen.*
262. *Test.*, p. 132, 528, 87-100.
263. *Religion and Philosophy*, c. 14.
264. Arthur Drews, *The Philosophy of Nietzsche.*
265. *Zarathustra.*
266. Hans Gallwitz, *Friederich Nietzsche, Ein Lebensbild.*
267. *L'Evolution Créatrice*, p. 198.
268. *Introduction to Metaphysics.*
269. *L'Evolution Créatrice*, p. 191.
270. *Annales de Philosophie Chrétienne*, March, 1922.
271. *Popular Science Monthly*, 1878.
272. Truth happens to an idea, it becomes true, is made true by events.
273. "On Pragmatic principles, if the hypothesis of God works satisfactorily in the widest sense of the word, it is true." *Pragmatism*, p. 299.